Disclaimer

This book is a philosophical exploration weaving together science, spirituality, contemplative traditions, and fiction. It touches on questions of consciousness, reality, and existence, but is not intended to provide final scientific answers, psychological advice, or religious instruction. Its purpose is to provoke reflection, encourage questioning, and open new pathways of thought.

References to quantum physics, neuroscience, and cosmology are presented in simplified form for philosophical exploration and should not be taken as formal scientific representations. Similarly, discussions inspired by non-dual traditions, such as *Advaita Vedanta*, are offered as interpretive reflections by the author—not as claims of personal realization or doctrinal authority.

All characters, dialogues, and situations are fictional unless explicitly stated otherwise. Any resemblance to actual persons, events, or experiences is coincidental. The views expressed belong to the author and are part of a broader philosophical and literary inquiry—not to be understood as empirical truth or spiritual testimony.

Readers are invited to approach the text with discernment, openness, and a spirit of inquiry. This book does not aim to deliver final answers but to inspire a deeper search for understanding.

CONSCIOUSNESS

The Theory of Everything

Science, Philosophy, and the Mystery of Consciousness

Nabaghan Ojha

ISBN : 978-93-5592-440-7

First Edition, 2025

Published by Nabaghan Ojha
Bhubaneswar, India

Author's Note

This book began not as an idea, but as a question that refused to fade: What is that one thing by which everything in the universe can be known, and every issue could be resolved?

Look around. Despite our astonishing progress, the human condition continues to become more and more difficult. People suffer not only from external crises, but from the weight of unlived lives—dreams deferred, identities diluted, meanings lost in the struggle for survival. Societies echo this pain. Mental health disorders surge. Families fragment. Empathy erodes. Communities fracture.

For minds like mine—restless, non-conforming, unwilling to settle—these questions are not philosophical luxuries. They are existential necessities. I searched for a lasting theory. Not just a scientific framework, but a truth that could heal the fractures within and around us. Could the long-sought **Theory of Everything**—if ever discovered—truly resolve these inner and outer crises?

That question led to the birth of this book.

Consciousness: The Theory of Everything is not a treatise. It is a mirror—held up to the soul, not the intellect. Through the journey of Ivaan, I have tried not to teach, but to awaken. This book is a remembrance, not a revelation. It whispers the ancient truth that each of us is infinitely more than the fractured image we carry of ourselves.

The path to this truth is neither straight nor simple. It demands that you listen—not with your ears, but with your soul. Amidst the noise of the world, where synthetic pleasures seduce and distractions derail, you must learn to hear the silent language of the universe. Its signs are subtle, its blessings disguised. Only a mind attuned to its inner calling can recognize them.

The universe is not passive—it conspires. It sends higher souls to guide you and then takes them away to test your solitude. It teaches quantum physics, neuroscience and metaphysics—not through textbooks, but through the raw experience of being. It plays with opposites: joy and sorrow, light and shadow, creation and destruction. It uses illusion as its brushstroke, painting trials that dissolve the ego and refine the spirit.

And then, when you are stripped bare, when your mind becomes still as a lake and sharp as lightning, it transforms into a superconductor—ready to receive the signals of real knowledge. In that moment, the veil lifts. The solution emerges. Not a theory, but a knowing. Not an answer, but a becoming.

This is the Theory of Everything—not written in equations, but etched in the silence between thoughts. It is the truth that lives within you, waiting to be remembered.

The book is an audacious attempt to weave together the three great threads of human understanding—science, philosophy and spirituality—into a single tapestry of truth. Not to compare them, but to unify them. Not to explain the universe, but to feel it, know it, and become it.

May this book not be an end, but a beginning. A quiet call to look within and find the dawn that never sets.

Thank you for daring to walk this path—with me, and within your own depths.

— Nabaghan Ojha

Contents

Prologue

"By whose will does the mind turn towards objects? By whose command does the breath begin? Who directs the tongue, the ear, the eye?"

So asked a disciple in a forest nearly ten thousand years ago. His words, preserved in the *Kena Upanishad*, still echo. The teacher's reply was no less enigmatic:

"It is the ear of the ear, the mind of the mind, the speech of speech, the life of life, the eye of the eye."

A riddle, not a solution—a signpost pointing inward, to that which animates perception yet lies beyond perception itself.

For centuries, this question has haunted human thought. Plato spoke of a reality higher than appearances. Descartes declared, "I think, therefore I am," but never pierced the mystery of the I. Laozi called it the Tao. The Buddha called it emptiness. Across cultures and ages, the same inquiry kept rising: **What is the source of consciousness?**

Today, the question haunts us more than ever. Neuroscience maps the firing of neurons with astonishing precision. Physics splits the atom, measures black holes, and searches for the first instant of creation. Artificial intelligence masters language, problem solving, and even art. Yet none of these conquests answer the question asked by the disciple in the forest.

Science can trace how light becomes vision, how sound becomes words, how memory takes form. But it cannot explain why there is an experiencer within. It can measure the brain when we see red, but not why red feels like red. It can track pain signals, but not why pain hurts. Machines now think faster than us, yet behind their brilliance there is no witness, no flame of awareness, no whisper of "I am."

The *Upanishadic* riddle slices through the heart of all this progress: **What is it that knows?**

Some insist consciousness is only an emergent flicker of matter—neurons firing in complexity. Others dare a more radical view: that consciousness is not an effect at all, but a foundation, as elemental as gravity or time.

And strange evidences unsettle old certainties. People clinically dead—no heartbeat, no brain activity—return with vivid accounts of awareness. Psychedelic research shows that when the brain's control centres fall silent, consciousness often expands, as though the mind were a filter rather than a generator. Quantum physics reveals entanglement and uncertainty, where the very act of observation seems to crystallize reality. Who, then, is the observer?

Perhaps the brain is not the origin, but the instrument—a receiver tuned to a field more vast than itself. Perhaps consciousness is not local at all, but woven through the fabric of existence—the hidden pulse of the cosmos.

If so, the disciple's question was not primitive curiosity. It was the first articulation of humanity's greatest challenge—one that science is beginning to face only now.

And why does it matter? Because our lives, our societies, our future may hinge upon it.

For all our progress, humanity remains strangely restless. Technology races ahead, and yet the inner emptiness deepens. Children scroll glowing screens late into the night, yet wake up lonelier than ever. The wealthy confess unease behind guarded walls, while the poor ache for meaning in the midst of suffering. We send machines to distant planets, but struggle to sit quietly with ourselves. The crises of our age—climate collapse, violence, despair—are not only failures of systems, but failures of self-understanding.

If consciousness is nothing more than an accidental spark in the machinery of matter, then value, purpose, and freedom dissolve into shadows—illusions with no lasting ground. But if consciousness is the very source from which matter arises—the unseen field in which stars burn and thoughts are born—then everything must change. Science must expand its foundation. Philosophy must widen its lens. Civilization itself must awaken to a new paradigm.

In this light, consciousness emerges not as a byproduct of evolution, but as the missing key—the unifier of what we thought were divided: mind and body, subject and object, matter and meaning. What physicists have sought in a single elegant equation, the sages hinted at in silence: that the true Theory of Everything is not written in symbols on a board, but discovered in the awareness that makes symbols possible in the first place.

And perhaps the greatest revelation is this: the answer we have searched for in the stars may already be here—hidden in the one place we rarely look—within the Self that asks the question.

It would not be another fact to memorize, nor another discovery to patent or weaponize. It would be a revelation that alters the very structure of knowing. For finding out what lies behind thought and breath is not an exercise to gain new information—it is to meet the source of information itself.

Such knowledge would not leave life untouched. It would dissolve all the old certainties. It would not merely change how we live—it would change what it means to be alive.

This is why the ancient question still matters. This is why it endures, even as empires rise and fall and galaxies spin their silent arcs. It is the one mystery that cannot be silenced, the one inquiry that outlives every answer we attempt to impose upon it.

Until it is faced, no progress will be whole. Until it is answered, no theory will be complete.

"By whose will does the mind turn towards thought?"

The forest has vanished. The master and disciple are long forgotten. Yet the question keeps burning—waiting like a hidden flame for the one who dares to draw near.

PART ONE

The Quantum Veil: Shadows of Perception

1

The Missing Star

The night had always been the same—endless, patient, vast—until the evening it wasn't. That night, the star that had watched over him for years simply failed to appear.

To everyone else, it was nothing more than a faint glimmer, one insignificant pinprick of light lost among countless others, swallowed by the immeasurable dark. A star among billions, barely noticed, soon forgotten in the endless scroll of night.

But to Ivaan, it was everything.

He never thought of it as a distant sun burning in silence without purpose. To him, it was alive—a pulse of love suspended in the heavens, the very soul of his mother transformed, watching him from afar with a tenderness deeper than words could hold. Perhaps it was the invention of a child desperate to anchor himself to love lost, or perhaps it was something older—a knowing that the world could never explain. He had been told the story once, when grief and wonder first collided within his young heart. His mind, eager for warmth, had embraced it like a sacred vow.

And with time, longing ripened into devotion.

Night after night, he would sit in the sky's quiet embrace, eyes fixed on that one unwavering point of light. He whispered to it—soft confessions, private joys, the raw ache of loneliness, and prayers woven from threads of hope and despair. The star listened. It never judged, never looked away, never betrayed him. It simply stood there—silent and steady—holding his words in its distant flame.

That single star became his confidant, his refuge, the keeper of his heart's secret landscapes. In its quiet, unwavering glow, he felt seen—completely, without condition, without the need for words. It bore witness to his dreams and his wounds alike, offering the only companionship that never faltered, never turned away. It did not demand perfection, nor did it ask for explanation. It simply remained, steady against the turning sky, as faithful as breath itself.

And in that silent bond, something began to awaken within him—something vast and unspoken. A subtle stirring in the spaces between breaths, between light and shadow, as if the universe whispered from its hidden chambers: that consciousness, far from being alone, was part of something immeasurable—a thread connecting all that ever was, all that ever would be.

No one knew of this nightly ritual except his father. And his father, with a wisdom tempered by sorrow and refined in silence, never questioned it. He understood what others might dismiss: that faith does not always ask for proof, that love, even when wrapped in illusion, can become more real than fact. For what is faith if not the courage to believe in what cannot be seen? What is grief if not the soul's attempt to weave eternity into a world where time steals everything precious?

In that star, Ivaan had found not just remembrance—but belonging. A fragile thread, yes—but one that bound the mortal heart to the eternal, the fleeting to the infinite. It gave him a sense of purpose, a quiet reassurance that his pain, his joy, his very existence were witnessed by something beyond himself.

But tonight… the star was gone.

The watcher of his solitude—the one constant in a world that shifted without warning—had vanished. It was as if an unseen hand had spread across the dark vault of the sky and plucked it from existence, erasing its light, its presence, its steady companionship. The heavens remained vast and indifferent. But to Ivaan, the sky felt hollow, bereft—as if a piece of his own soul had been torn away and cast into the void.

What is eternal then, if even the sky betrays its promises? What is truth, if the very light we lean on disappears without warning? The absence of a star was no simple loss of brightness—it was the shattering of certainty itself.

A tremor rose in Ivaan's chest as he lowered himself to the cold earth. His small frame seemed swallowed by the vast silence of the valley, as though the night itself held its breath in pity—or indifference. If the soul is immortal, how could the star—his mother's star, the flame that carried her presence across the darkness—be extinguished? Was immortality nothing more than a tale the living told themselves, a balm for the heart against the harshness of endings?

The sky stretched endlessly above him, hollow and unfeeling. The other stars glittered on, distant and aloof, their sharp points of light scattered like careless thoughts across the heavens. Nothing had changed for them. Nothing had been lost. But for Ivaan, the void carved itself into the night like an open wound—dark, aching, raw.

He stared until his eyes burned, willing it back into being—as if longing, fierce and unwavering, could reverse the decree written by fate or time. But the darkness remained unmoved.

It felt wrong in a way words could not capture. Not the ache of losing a thing—but the terror of losing something deeper: a truth upon which his heart had leaned for so long. And if the sky itself could erase what seemed eternal, then what else might vanish without warning? What other promises might crumble in silence, leaving nothing but emptiness in their place?

The questions rose within him like a restless tide—recurring and relentless.

Why does love blaze with such intensity, only to fade by the first light of the morning? Why does death visit the innocent, while the corrupt walk nonchalantly beneath the same sky? Why must beauty bloom besides suffering, its petals trembling in the same wind that carries sorrow? Why is there a universe— an expanse so vast, so radiant — at all? And why does simply being alive bring pain?

These questions battered his mind, returning again and again like waves against rocks, each crest heavier than the last.

Change had always frightened him. Even as a child, he had recoiled from it instinctively—as if it carried with it the sting of betrayal. People changed. His mother, once the warmest shelter of his small world, had vanished when he needed her the most. Friends who had laughed with him beneath the open sky now turned their faces away without reason. Storms swept through the valley, ripping roofs off homes, uprooting trees, and scattering memories like broken glass. Neighbours who once filled the air with song now moved with bent backs and hollow silence, as if grief had settled upon their shoulders.

Perhaps, deep within, he had always known the truth: that life was a tide that takes more than it gives. But that knowledge had never softened the blow. To know something is one thing; to accept it is something entirely different. His heart, stubborn and yearning, refused to bow to what it could not understand.

That night, long after the village had sunk into sleep, Ivaan rose quietly and stepped outside. The mountains stood like dark sentinels, their jagged ridges cutting sharply into the deeper black of the sky. The air was cool and fragrant with the scent of pine and damp earth. Somewhere far below, the river murmured its endless hymn, as if offering comfort to the night itself.

He searched the sky again, his eyes locked on the empty space where the star had always shone. Surely it was a mistake. Surely the night would relent, soften, and return what it had stolen. Surely… But the heavens remained silent—vast, indifferent, unmoved by his longing.

A sudden gust of wind swept through the trees, rattling dry leaves, that sounded like brittle whispers. It carried with it a cold, unforgiving certainty: nothing—not even what you believe is eternal—is safe from change.

With a slow, reluctant breath, Ivaan turned back toward the house. Inside, the dim lamp flickered against the wooden walls, its weak light pushing shadows that stretched and recoiled like restless spirits—alive, unsettled, waiting.

He sprawled himself on the bed, but the darkness behind his closed eyes was far heavier than the one outside. The missing star returned to him again and again—not as a glimmer of light, but as a question sharpened by absence. It felt unbearably personal, like a wound that would not heal.

What else in his life was already fading, quietly slipping away—waiting to be noticed—only when it was gone?

He thought of the girl at school who, without warning, had stopped speaking to him—her laughter gone, her eyes turned elsewhere, as if he had vanished from her world overnight. He thought of his mother's sudden absence, leaving an ache far deeper than the empty space in the sky. He thought of neighbours who once filled the air with song, now stooped by invisible burdens, their faces lined with a sense of resignation.

It wasn't merely that things changed. It was that they changed without reason, without mercy—shifting like sand beneath his feet, as if the universe rewrote its rules while he was still learning to play by the old rules.

That night, sleep eluded him. Instead, something deeper stirred within—something neither hope nor despair, but a quiet, persistent hunger. Not yet the light of purpose—but an ache that could not be ignored. If answers existed, they had to lie somewhere beyond the mountains that hemmed him in. And if there were none... he needed to face that truth as well.

The question pulsed through him like a second heartbeat: What is this life, if it can vanish without warning? The darkness outside seemed to breathe with him, waiting for the moment when doubt would give way to the journey that lay ahead.

By dawn, the valley was shrouded in a soft, ghostly mist. The river flowed low and steady, as if nothing had changed. The mountains stood firm, their peaks rising into the pale sky as they always had. Life, on the surface, appeared untouched.

But for Ivaan, everything had shifted. The landscape remained whole, yet it felt hollowed out—like a painting—which has its brightest colour stripped off—leaving only outlines and a shadow.

He stood at the threshold of his home, eyes fixed on the ridge where the star once glowed gently. The morning light stretched across the sky, soft and pale, but the emptiness remained—throbbing like a hidden wound only he could see, a silence that clung to his chest and, refused to let go.

Most boys, the world would say, would grieve for a while and then forget—returning to their routines, letting time dull the pain, allowing habit and distraction to bury the loss. But Ivaan could not. His heart carried questions far beyond his years, sharp as blades, restless as the wind.

Perhaps such souls are rare—marked not by choice, but by some silent decree of the universe. A hidden current seems to pull them towards moments that fracture the ordinary and demand a deeper sight. Some call it destiny, others karma, and still others grace. Whatever the name, the force is the same: the world refuses to let them drift back into forgetfulness. It summons them towards what lies beyond the veil.

For Ivaan, the vanishing star was no accident; it was a summons. Life itself had spoken, and he could no longer pretend not to hear.

Somewhere deep within him, a thought took root—dangerous in its clarity, pure in its simplicity: If the answers are not here—I must go where they are.

It was not courage that stirred him, nor the thrill of adventure. It was something more urgent, more profound—a refusal to remain in a world that erased what he loved without reason, that offered no explanation for the sudden void left behind.

The mountains had raised him, their peaks and valleys cradling his childhood like a gentle, caring hand. But they could not hold him any longer. The missing star had torn a seam in his heart, unstitched the certainty that once bound him to the familiar. Now, every path he knew felt too narrow, and every routine too small. The world he had trusted no longer seemed whole.

Something larger called to him from beyond the ridge, beyond the river, beyond even the silence of the sky. He did not yet know where that call would lead—but he knew he could not turn away.

2

The Shifting World

The absence of the star had thrown a question into him. But long before that night, the mountains themselves had been whispering their riddles. Their silence was not empty; it was alive, older than memory, patient as stone. Ivaan was just a boy when he first felt it—the weight of a stillness that seemed to know him before he knew himself.

He lived with his father, Ayaan, in a forgotten village cradled in the lap of Kashmir, not far from Pahalgam. It was a place that carried the breath of ancient seekers and sages, where meadows remembered footsteps long vanished and the winds seemed to murmur secrets from the other side of history.

Their home was humble, stitched together with mud, stone, and the rhythm of routine. But the landscape surrounding them—the chinar-lined trails, the snow-fed streams, and the brooding pine forests—was anything but ordinary. This was no mere village; it was a cradle of stillness, the kind that changes a person just by being in it.

Ayaan was a shepherd—not by choice, but by necessity. His ancestors had tended flocks for generations, borrowing sheep from wealthier peasants and leading them to summer grazing pastures, only to return them before the harshness of winter descended. Ayaan had once dreamed of a life in academia. He was well-read, curious and drawn to the mysteries of existence. But life, with its quiet force, had nudged him down another path. Over time, what had begun as reluctant duty transformed into a calling. He no longer saw himself as just a herder of sheep; he saw himself as a guardian of a rhythm older than civilization, a keeper of something sacred.

During the grazing season, he would retreat to a small hut in the high meadows. Occasionally, Ivaan joined him. The days spent there felt like stepping into another world. He would walk beside his father in silence, watching him read the clouds as if they were scriptures, listening keenly as Ayaan spoke to the animals in a mixed language of gestures, breaths, and stillness. There was no need for words between them; silence spoke volumes.

At night, under the vast, ink-blue sky, Ivaan would lie beside his father. Ayaan's stories drifted into the darkness like smoke—tales— not of kings or warriors—but of rivers that remembered, winds that healed, and stars that had names older than memory. He spoke of spirits in the hills, of listening rather than knowing, of a world within the world. It was in those quiet moments, beneath the stars, that Ivaan first felt the tug of something deeper—an unnamed ache to understand not just the world, but what it meant to be.

Back in the village, Ivaan had just completed his schooling—Class XII—at a modest school two valleys away. He had a curious mind and a tender heart, traits his teachers noted and praised. Yet, the weight of his family's reality hung like the mist in the morning: silent, inevitable. Higher education required resources they didn't possess. His father's earnings, steady but meagre, couldn't stretch to cover college. Dreams, he was beginning to understand, do not always bloom.

Neither father nor son spoke of it. There was nothing to say. They moved through their days with a quiet grace, the love between them unspoken but understood. Sometimes, a dream is mourned not with tears but with silence—a silence that becomes a part of one's breath.

One day, purely on impulse, Ivaan began learning the ways of the flock. He studied their patterns, their hunger, their seasons. He learned the language of the wind and the weight of the sky. It wasn't that he had surrendered to a life among sheep; it was just that he had begun preparing himself for the life he feared might well be his only option.

But in the hidden space between dusk and dawn, something else stirred in him. He didn't yet have a name for it. But it was there—a restlessness, a question, a longing.

And somewhere deep inside, Ayaan knew that his son, though he continued to walk beside him, was not meant to follow in his footsteps.

By the time Ivaan turned eighteen, he had become part of the landscape itself—his skin bronzed by the sun, his gait easy and sure across rocks and ridges. The sharp winds had sculpted his face into angles of quiet strength. There was no trace left of the boy who once stumbled through the meadows in awe. Now, he moved like someone who belonged, not merely to the land, but to its memory.

The sheep responded to him with instinctive trust. He had learned not just their patterns, but their personalities—the stubbornness of one, the timidity of the other. His voice carried a calm authority, firm and kind, and his touch held a steadiness born of deep attention. He had memorised the secret veins of the valley: where the wild mint grew nourished by hidden springs, where the fog settled thickest before rain, and where the cliffs cast shadows—like the hands of old gods.

For Ivaan, the valley had become more than home; it was an unspoken scripture. The wind taught him patience. The river taught him persistence. The silence between birdsong taught him how to listen—not with ears, but with something deeper.

But for Ayaan, each day brought a quiet ache. He watched helplessly as his son kept sliding into the kind of life he had once dreamed of sparing him from. The boy, who once spoke of books and cities, now spoke in the language of the wild. Still, Ayaan kept comforting himself with the hope that Ivaan would come around one day. He knew that shepherding was not just about tending sheep. It was about reading danger in the curve of the sky, in the sudden hush before a storm. The valley, for all its beauty, could turn against you without warning. Wolves prowled the higher slopes, unseen but present. And the snow—when it came early—was like a wall falling from the heavens.

Ayaan had seen enough to know that survival here was not a matter of strength, but of listening. Truly listening. And so, though his bones ached more than they once did, he resolved to walk alongside Ivaan for one more season. He would not release his son until he was certain the boy had learned to listen—not just to the land, but to himself.

Each evening, when the long day folded into twilight, shepherds gathered around their fires in small clusters, trading stories as old as the hills—tales of lost sheep, near-deaths, strange lights in the forests, and omens read in broken twigs and sudden silences.

Among them, Ayaan held quiet authority. He was not the loudest, but when he spoke, the others listened with rapt attention. His words were shaped by experience and tempered by something rarer—understanding. He never mocked fear, never dismissed superstition. Instead, he translated it. For those listening, he was a bridge between old wisdom and silent reason.

Ivaan often sat on the edge of these gatherings—half in, half out. He spoke little. His eyes wandered to the sky more often than to the circle of men. His questions, when they came, were different. While the others asked about weather patterns and grazing routes, Ivaan asked why the river never flowed the same way twice? Why some places felt sacred for no reason? Why the wind sometimes carried a sadness that had no source?

The others smiled indulgently, unsure what to make of him. But Ayaan never dismissed their questions. He answered them the best he could—with patience, with metaphor, and with love. He knew those questions didn't come from boredom or fantasy. They came from the place where longing lives— the birthplace of true seekers.

Some people are chosen by the world. Others are chosen by the unknown.

Perhaps the universe, in its unfathomable grace, had chosen Ivaan. Not because he was special in any visible way, but because he listened. Because he had learned to see without demanding meaning, and to wonder without seeking answers.

And perhaps the universe, in its quiet intelligence, had chosen Ayaan too—not merely as a father by blood, but as a father of spirit. A man whose own dreams had once scattered like autumn leaves across the windswept ridges, only to return, glinting anew in his son's eyes.

Ayaan was no longer just a shepherd of sheep. He had become a guide who held the lantern not in front, but behind—offering light without leading, letting Ivaan walk into the dark and find his own footing.

He knew this land better than most: the temper of the sky, the signs on the wind, the shape of storms before they arrived. But now, he was teaching Ivaan—not by lecture, but through experience. Each lesson in the wild was both about survival and something deeper. The valley was not just a backdrop; it was a force, a consciousness. It revealed itself only to those willing to wait and watch.

"Watch the shadows," Ayaan once said as they walked through an ancient grove. "They'll tell you more than the light ever will."

He taught Ivaan how to read the trail—not just the obvious prints, but the faint tremor in disturbed soil, the subtle break of a twig. "See here?" Ayaan crouched, brushing aside a veil of leaves. "A wolf passed through this place. The earth keeps no secrets from those who listen."

Silence was his oldest ally. In the hush before dawn, when the mist clung to the peaks, or in the stillness just after twilight when even the wind seemed to pause—Ayaan listened. And in silence, he heard things most people missed.

"There are many kinds of silence," he told Ivaan by the fire one evening. "The silence before the rain. The silence when two hearts understand each other. And the silence that comes when wisdom arrives. It comes quietly, without any noise."

Most feared silence, mistaking it for emptiness. But Ayaan had long learned that silence was not void—it was depth. "If you cannot sit with silence," he once said, "you cannot sit with yourself. And if you cannot sit with yourself, you will never truly know who you are."

Their days followed the rhythm of the land. Ivaan walked beside his father, watching and absorbing. He began to notice how the sheep grew uneasy before a storm, how the dogs lifted their heads long before the wind shifted. Ayaan observed quietly, nodding when Ivaan got it right.

"One day," Ayaan said as they crossed a narrow ridge, "you'll feel these changes in your skin, not just on your eyes. Trust that."

On another trail, where the path thinned into broken stones, Ayaan stopped. "Look," he said, pointing to what seemed like an unmarked slope. Ivaan frowned. "There's nothing." Ayaan smiled. "Look again." And suddenly, Ivaan saw it—the faint line of flattened grass, the worn edges of rock. A hidden path. "The clearest road isn't always the truest one," Ayaan said. "You must learn to see what others pass by."

Their conversations were few, but heavy with meaning. In one such moment, Ayaan sat beside Ivaan as the stars blinked through the dark. "Fire, my son," he said, "is like the spirit inside you. A spark can warm, protect, guide. But let it burn unchecked, and it will consume you. Anger, desire, ambition—they are flames. Master them, or they will master you."

And then came the quietest but hardest lesson of all.

"Nothing stays the same, Ivaan," Ayaan murmured one night as the cold stars glinted above. "The rivers shift, the mountains wear down, the flock will grow and vanish in time. Do not cling. Holding on too tightly is like grasping water; the harder you try, the faster it escapes."

Ivaan did not speak. But something settled in him—something clear and quiet. He understood now that being a shepherd was not merely the tending of sheep. It was a metaphor for life itself. It was about waiting without anxiety. Protecting without controlling. Listening beyond words.

In those silent walks, beneath a sky larger than time, he had learned to trust the invisible—to find wisdom not in answers, but in presence.

And in that stillness, he was beginning—not just to become a shepherd—but to become himself.

One evening, as they watched the twilight dissolve into darkness, Ayaan spoke again. "The world is always in motion, Ivaan. But a shepherd's strength is not in resisting change—it is in walking with it. Learn to see impermanence not as loss, but as the rhythm of life. In letting go, we discover a deeper kind of holding—one that does not bind, but frees."

Ivaan listened, his heart both heavy and light. He understood now that being a shepherd was not just about tending a flock—it was about tending to life itself. And in the quiet wisdom of the mountains, he had learned not just how to survive, but how to see, listen, and trust the journey ahead.

But one morning, everything changed.

The flock had wandered towards the northern ridge—an area they rarely visited. Ivaan, drawn by a strange urgency, followed them. The mist was heavier than usual, and the familiar trail seemed altered, as if the earth had shifted in its sleep. He called out to the sheepdog, but it went unresponded.

Then he saw it—a shadow across the ridge, too tall to be a sheep—too fidgety to be a rock. A wolf, perhaps. Or something else.

He turned to call for his father, but Ayaan was nowhere in sight.

Panic rose in his chest; a chill, quite distinct from the mountain wind creeping into his bones, swept through his veins. He moved forward, unsure whether he was chasing danger or being led into it. And then, just as the sun broke through the fog, he saw it: a patch of scorched earth, fresh and black—where fire had touched what should never burn. A strange symbol was etched into the ash—unfamiliar, deliberate, and almost ceremonial.

It wasn't just nature testing him anymore. Something else had stirred—something neither man nor mountain had taught him to face.

By the time Ayaan reached him, Ivaan was crouched near the burned patch, silent, eyes wide. Ayaan placed a hand on his shoulder, but said nothing. His face, usually calm, now bore a flicker of something Ivaan had never seen before—worry, yes, but more than that, recognition.

"You weren't supposed to find this," Ayaan whispered, barely audible. "Not yet."

Ivaan turned to him. "What is it?"

Ayaan looked away, towards the distant horizon where the mist began to lift. "A sign," he said. "That you don't need me to lead your journey anymore."

And in that moment, Ivaan knew: his path was no longer just about mastering the mountains, or even himself. Something deeper had begun to unfold—an inheritance not just of land or lineage, but of a secret older than both. The silence would not be enough now. He would have to ask the questions no one else had dared to raise.

Over time, Ivaan evolved. He was no longer merely a shepherd tending to his flock. He had become something quieter and more radiant—a watchful guide attuned to the hidden rhythms of the world. His wisdom did not come from books or doctrines. It arose from presence, from walking the land with open senses and a listening heart. When Ivaan spoke, people felt something shift inside them—as though the earth itself had paused to hear him.

He noticed what others overlooked: the breath held by the wind before clouds amassed; the hush that descended before the first snowflake touched the valley floor; the stillness of the river before it changed its course. Nature was not scenery to him—it was a living intelligence, a patient mentor, a mirror that reflected truths buried in the soul. The mountains whispered endurance. The rain chanted surrender. The river hummed transformation.

One afternoon, as he guided the flock along a familiar slope, the light dimmed with startling suddenness. The wind turned sharp, impatient. Thunder muttered in the distance. The golden sheen of the hills darkened beneath a sky swollen with impending rain. Then it broke—not in a gentle drizzle, but in a fury. The heavens roared, the earth trembled beneath torrents of water, and chaos unfurled across the valley.

Shepherds shouted over the wind, egging on their flocks towards shelter, boots slipping in the mud. Through the swirling storm, a small figure tripped—falling to the earth with a cry. A young shepherd boy, no more than twelve, had cut his knee on jagged stone.

The others hesitated, worry flickering across their faces. "Aarav!" someone called, the voice barely audible in the downpour.

That name—Aarav—settled in Ivaan's heart like an echo returning after years. He watched the boy rise slowly, limping but determined. Something stirred in Ivaan, more than compassion. It was recognition. A thread had tugged, invisible but strong.

Later that evening, the valley breathed in silence again. Stars shimmered over the moist earth, and the distant crackle of a fire drifted in the breeze. Ivaan sat beside his father outside their modest cottage, wrapped in a silence that was both shared and solitary.

Ayaan sipped his tea slowly, his eyes resting on the shadowed silhouette of the mountains. The firelight danced in his beard, but his gaze remained still, as though listening to something deeper than sound.

Ivaan's voice emerged gently, like mist rising from the land: "Father… why do people call me Ivaan? If I had been given another name, would I still be the same?"

Ayaan turned to him, brows lifting gently—not in surprise, but in solemn acknowledgment. The question wasn't strange. Children often ask about names, about identity. But there was something in Ivaan's eyes—something weightier than mere curiosity. It wasn't a game. It wasn't wonder for its own sake. It was a real question, born from something he had seen that afternoon, something he couldn't yet name.

For a few moments, Ayaan said nothing. The stillness between them deepened. Then he set his cup down and looked not at his son, but at the ground between them—as if looking for the root from which a true answer might rise.

At last, he spoke.

"My son… if I asked you to bring water from the lake, what would you do?"

Ivaan, thoughtful and alert, responded without hesitation: "I would take a vessel, walk to the lake, fill it, and bring it back. That's what I always do."

Ayaan smiled, faintly. His eyes now met Ivaan's, clear and unwavering.

"And if I gave you a clay pot, a copper bowl, or even a wooden ladle… would the water be any different?"

Ivaan frowned slightly, then shook his head.

"No, the water will be the same."

Ayaan nodded slowly.

"Names are like vessels, Ivaan. They carry something. But they are not the thing itself. You could be called Aarav, Kian, or Zahir. What matters is the water inside—the being. The name is for others. But you must come to know the one who carries the name."

Ayaan smiled softly, nodding. "Yes, exactly. To fetch water, you need a vessel. Without it, the water slips through your fingers and returns to the lake. The vessel gives shape to something that, by its nature, has none."

He paused, allowing the thought to settle in the stillness between them.

"In the same way, my son," he continued, "in this world of form and function, of action and interaction, we carry names as vessels. Ivaan is your vessel. It allows others to know you, to call you, to find you, to relate to you. Just as the container holds water, your name holds the stories people tell about you. But the container is not the water—and your name is not who you are."

Ivaan's eyes followed the shadows of the trees swaying gently in the moonlight, and something within him stirred.

"We are born into names," Ayaan said, his voice now quieter, "but we are not born as names. The name is given. The being is already there."

He picked up a small pebble and rolled it between his fingers.

"There was a time before anyone called you anything—and yet, you were there. You breathed. You felt the sun on your skin and the pull of hunger in your belly. Existence does not need a name. The bird sings without knowing it is called a bird. The wind moves through the valleys with no name for itself. The stars shine nameless, yet they've lit the skies for ages."

Ayaan looked at his son and placed a gentle hand on his shoulder.

"Names are needed in the world for trade and talk. But if you close your eyes and go inward, you will find a place where no one calls you anything and yet, you are more fully yourself than ever. That is your true self—not the name that echoes in the world, but the presence that watches silently behind your eyes."

Ivaan was quiet for a while. Then, with a voice barely above a whisper, as though he was afraid the night might shatter the delicate thread between them, he asked:

"Then… what is real in this world?"

Ayaan smiled—not out of amusement, but out of recognition. The question wasn't ordinary. It was the kind that ripens slowly in silent minds. A question that signals a turning inward.

He stirred the tea in his cup, and said:

"Ah, the question that unravels a thousand lifetimes."

He looked towards the mountains—dark, unmoving silhouettes beneath the canopy of stars. The air around them was crisp, the silence sacred.

"My son, look at the flame of that lantern," he said, pointing toward the soft glow flickering inside their small hut. "Its light touches everything in the room—your face, my face, the walls, the books. But if someone asks what is real—the light, or the things it reveals—what would you say?"

Ivaan paused for a while, immersed in thoughtful silence. And then, he said; "Both seem real. But without the light, I wouldn't see anything. So maybe… the light is what makes them real to me?"

Ayaan nodded, pleased.

"Exactly. Now imagine this world—its people, mountains, rivers, joys, and sorrows—all as objects revealed by a light. That light is your awareness, your consciousness. It touches everything you know, yet it itself cannot be touched. Everything you call 'real' appears in that light, but the light itself is never seen. It just—is."

He paused.

"Forms change. Names change. Bodies age and fall. But that which is aware of all this—that silent witness within you—remains unchanged. It has no beginning, no end. That, my son, is the only reality."

Ivaan looked up at the sky, where stars blinked through the cold air like eyes watching from eternity.

"So… all that we see is like the shadows on the wall?"

Ayaan smiled again. "Not shadows… but reflections. Like the moon reflecting the sun's light. The world reflects reality, but it is not the reality itself. The real is not what appears and disappears. The real is what never changes."

Silence returned between them—not empty, but full. Full of stars. Full of presence. Full of a truth that did not require any words.

Ayaan continued, "The unreal has no true existence. It neither existed before time began, nor will it exist after time has faded. And because it does not have an existence independent of time, it does not truly exist even now—though it appears it does."

"Let me explain with an example. Think of a dream. While you are dreaming, everything seems real. You see people, places, and events unfolding before you. You may feel joy, fear, or sorrow. In those moments, it all seems completely true."

A sudden cry of a night-bird pierced through the valley's silence. Ivaan's heart jumped, clinging to that sound as proof that this world was solid, not a phantom. Yet, even as the echo faded into the darkness, he felt a chill: could this too be no more than a passing dream?

His father's voice carried on, calm and steady. "But the moment you wake up, what happens? The entire dream vanishes as if it never existed. You cannot hold on to it, nor can you go back and live in it again. It was real only as long as you were asleep. But did it have any real existence of its own? No. The moment you awoke, its apparent existence dissolved into nothingness."

Ivaan nodded slightly, his brows furrowed in thought.

"This world," Ayaan continued, "is not much different from a dream. It appears real while we are caught in it, just as a dream feels real while we are dreaming. But anything that ceases to exist upon deeper realization cannot be truly real. The wise ones say that the world is like a mirage—an illusion that tricks the eye, but vanishes upon closer examination. Imagine walking in a desert on a hot day. From a distance, you see what appears to be water shimmering on the horizon. Your eyes perceive it, your mind believes it, and you may even feel the thirst that urges you to run toward it. But as you get closer, the illusion fades. The water was never there to begin with."

Ivaan's eyes flickered with curiosity. "But, Father, if the world is unreal, then why do we experience it so vividly? Why do we feel joy, sorrow, love, and pain if they don't truly exist?"

The question hung in the night air, heavier than silence itself. Ayaan did not answer at once. He looked at his son with an intensity that seemed to reach beyond the boy's words, as though he were not only hearing the question, but also weighing the soul that had asked it. His gaze was steady, patient, almost searching—as if the truth itself was waiting to see if Ivaan was ready.

Between them, silence stretched. But it was no ordinary silence. It was alive, filled with the echo of something unspoken. The fire crackled softly, the river whispered far below and the vast mountains seemed to lean closer, holding their breath as if they, too, awaited the reply.

3
The Unseen Ground

At last, Ayaan spoke, his voice low and measured, as though he did not wish to disturb the silence but only carry it forward.

"The world feels vivid, Ivaan, because our minds are trained to chase shadows and mistake them for substance. Joy and sorrow, love, and pain—they seem to rise and fall like waves, but waves are never separate—from the ocean beneath. What we feel is not false; it is incomplete. To see only the wave, and not the water, is to be deceived by appearances."

He reached down, picked up a handful of soil, and let it crumble slowly between his fingers. "Look at this earth. From it, a thousand forms arise—trees, flowers, fruits, even our bodies. They change, they wither, they vanish. But the earth remains. The wise ones call it the ground—the essence beneath form. It is always here, whether or not we notice it."

Ivaan's brow furrowed. "But how do we know what is ground and what is only form?"

Ayaan smiled faintly. He picked up a small stone and traced a circle in the dirt. "Think of clay, my son. A potter takes clay and shapes it into pots, bowls, and vases. They have different names, different uses. But what are they, really? Only clay. Break the pot, and the clay remains. The form is lost, but the essence is untouched. In the same way, all this"—he gestured to the mountains, the river, even their own bodies—"is nothing but form. What remains beneath it is the unseen ground."

Ivaan sat quietly, his eyes following the faint curve his father had drawn in the dirt. The words did not give him certainty, but they pressed against something within, as though awakening a memory older than himself.

Ayaan smiled again, knowing the next question was inevitable. "The answer lies in understanding the nature of reality itself," he said. "Take the example of a movie. When you sit in a theatre, you see characters laughing, crying, fighting, and loving. You feel emotions rising within you. Your heart may race in excitement, or tears may well up in your eyes."

Ivaan thought of the missing star. How could something so constant, so trusted, dissolve as though it had never been? His chest tightened. If the heavens could play tricks, what else was a projection?

Ayaan's voice drew him back. "And yet, all of it is just light—projected on a screen. None of it is real. But while the movie is playing, it completely absorbs you. It is only when the film ends, or when you step out of the theatre, that you remember—it was all just an illusion."

Ayaan let the words settle before continuing, "This world is like that. It seems real because we are within it, just as a dream seems real while we are dreaming. But its reality is borrowed—it does not have an independent, permanent existence. That which is truly real must be eternal, unchanging, and ever-present. But everything in this world is constantly changing. Our bodies change, the seasons change, and even the mountains, which seem solid and immovable, will one day crumble and disappear. If something can be destroyed, it means it was never truly real."

Ayaan paused, looking at Ivaan to see if he was following. Ivaan's face showed deep contemplation, as if he were seeing the world differently for the first time.

"That which is real," Ayaan concluded, his voice now a whisper against the vast silence, "must always exist, independent of time and space. It cannot be created, nor destroyed. And if you search for something that fits this definition, you will find only one thing remains—awareness itself. The one who sees. The one who knows. The one who is untouched by all change. That alone is real. Everything else," he said with calm certainty, "is a passing shadow."

A hush settled between them. Even the wind seemed to hold its breath; the crackle of the fire remained the only sound. The valley stretched out like a canvas of stillness, the peaks now dressed in silver moonlight. It felt as if even the mountains leaned in, listening.

For the first time, Ivaan's gaze wavered.

He turned his eyes to the distant ridgelines, his thoughts spiralling inward. If the world around him was but an illusion, what was the reality he had yet to wake up to? The question didn't just intrigue him—it unsettled him. Beneath his calm exterior, something stirred. Not wonder this time, but resistance.

"But Father," he said slowly, his voice threaded with a quiet urgency, "for people like us, this world is everything. We wake up to it. We build dreams in it. We fall in love. We suffer when those we love are hurt. We rejoice when they smile. How can I pretend it's unreal when I feel it so deeply? When loss breaks our hearts, or joy lifts us beyond ourselves—how can that be an illusion?"

His voice trembled slightly, not from fear, but from the weight of what he wanted to protect: the tangible world, the raw beauty of relationships, the warmth of presence, the grief of parting.

He looked into his father's eyes—not in defiance, but with an unspoken need to understand.

Ayaan didn't answer at once. He heard not just the words, but the human ache behind them. He shifted closer, his expression softening.

"My son," he began, his voice slow and anchoring, "I hear the truth in your words. This world feels real because we live inside it, breathe it, love within it. And to say it is not real feels almost cruel. But the sages never said the world doesn't exist. What they taught is more subtle: the world exists—but not in the way we think. In the final analysis, it is not real."

He let the pause hang, then added, “Let me try to show you.”

He picked up a twig and traced a curve in the dirt. “Imagine a man walking at dusk. He sees a rope, but in the dim light, his mind mistakes it for a snake. Fear strikes—his heart races. He panics. But then someone brings a lamp, and the illusion disappears. The snake was never there, but its power was real—as long as it was believed.”

Ivaan pressed his palm against the ground beside him. The earth felt cold, rough, unyielding. Was his father truly saying that even the soil, the trees, his own breath could be no more than a mistake of the mind? His chest tightened at the thought.

Ayaan’s eyes caught the flicker of doubt on his son’s face. He continued softly, “That’s what the world is like to the unenlightened mind. It seems real, so it hurts. But what if—just like the snake—it’s only an illusion? What if, behind it, lies something untouched?”

Ivaan’s face was unreadable. Ayaan sensed his mind grappling with the truth, but his heart still holding on to the visible world.

So, he tried again.

“The potter takes clay,” he said, picking up a stone, “and shapes it into pots, vases, and bowls. Different names, different uses.”

Ivaan’s gaze drifted to the old wooden cup beside his father, its rim marked by a faint crack—a fracture waiting to deepen. For the first time, he saw it not as an object of use, but as something fragile—already dissolving into what it once was. A sudden unease twisted in his gut.

Ayaan rolled the stone in his palm. “But they’re all just clay. Break the pot, the clay remains. What changes is the form. What stays is the essence.”

He looked at Ivaan with quiet intensity.

"Everything you see—your body, my body, the house, the pain of loss, the sweetness of love—all are forms. Beautiful, yes. Powerful, certainly. But temporary. The deeper reality, like the clay, never leaves. It just hides behind the form."

Ayaan reclined slightly, his gaze lingering on his son's furrowed brow.

"Have you ever had a dream so vivid," he asked, "that, while dreaming, you believed it was real? You ran, you laughed, you cried—you felt joy and sorrow, as if it were all happening to you?"

Ivaan nodded gently, eyes narrowed in recollection.

"But then," Ayaan continued, "you woke up. And the dream vanished—just like that. The pain of the loss, the joy of the gain—gone. No weight remained. That is how this world is, my son. It appears real because we are still inside it. But when we 'wake up', when our awareness shifts to a higher truth, we will see it for what it really is: a phase, a fleeting appearance, like the mist under the morning sun."

Ivaan's lips parted as if to speak, but Ayaan raised a hand gently, gesturing him to listen further.

"Let me share a story," he said, His voice settled into the measured cadence of an age-old tale

"One evening, Janaka, the King of ancient Mithila, sat alone after a long day of ruling his kingdom. Exhaustion overcame him, and he drifted into sleep. In his dream, he was no longer a king, but a beggar—barefoot, hungry, lost in a land that did not know him. The sun scorched his skin. He knocked on doors, pleaded for food, but was turned away again and again."

Ivaan's face tensed, the imagery gripping him.

"Eventually, he stumbled upon a small hut. The kind villagers took him in and gave him a bowl of rice. With trembling hands, he reached for it—just then, a clap of thunder shattered the sky. He woke up, back in his silken bed, his palace intact, attendants nearby."

Ayaan paused, letting the contrast settle.

"But his heart was pounding. The hunger and the pain—they had felt real. He asked himself: Which world is true? The one I woke into—or the one I just left behind? The dream had vanished, yes—but so had the dream of kingship during his time as a beggar."

Ivaan's eyes glinted with uncertainty. Ayaan could sense it—the pull between the known and the unknowable.

"Janaka summoned his sages," Ayaan went on. "They gave him wise words, but none satisfied his doubt. Until Sage Ashtavakra arrived."

He drew closer, his voice soft but certain.

"When Janaka asked, 'Which one is real—the dream or the waking?' Ashtavakra replied, 'Neither is real. When you dreamed, the beggar's world was all you knew—this palace did not exist. Now, the dream is gone, but the palace too shall fade. You are not the king. You are not the beggar. You are the one who witnessed both. That alone is real.'"

The wind whispered through the trees as dry leaves fluttered down, catching the moonlight like falling embers.

Ivaan sat very still, the story piercing into him like an arrow. Something inside him resisted—yet something deeper stirred. He wanted to believe his father. But to let go of the tangible world, even in thought, felt like unmooring his very sense of self.

"But…" he began, then stopped. His throat was dry.

Ayaan saw the hesitation. "It's not easy," he said. "This truth isn't meant to be swallowed whole. It must be chewed, lived, reflected upon—until one day, you do not just hear it, but see it."

He placed a hand on Ivaan's shoulder.

"For now, just remember: you are the witness. Everything else—dream or reality—is the stage."

Ivaan was silent. His father's words made sense—but they also unsettled something deeply entrenched within him. Everything he had believed, everything he had trusted—the solidity of the world, the importance of success, the fear of loss—was now being crushed under the weight of a truth that felt both profound and elusive.

Sensing the inner storm behind his son's composed expression, Ayaan softened his tone and offered an everyday metaphor.

"Think of a movie playing on a screen," he said gently. "The scenes change—there is love, war, happiness, sadness—but the screen itself never changes. No matter what happens in the movie, the screen remains untouched. This world is like that movie, and our true self—our awareness—is like the screen. We get caught up in the drama of life. But when we step back, we realize that the screen remains unchanged. Just as our true self remains untouched by the passing scenes of joy and sorrow."

He placed a firm, warm hand on Ivaan's shoulder. "My son, the world is not completely false—but it is not the highest truth either. It is ever-changing, impermanent, and therefore not the ultimate reality. What is real? That which never changes. That which remains even when everything else fades. That which was never born and nor will ever die. That is the true reality—the eternal consciousness, the self, the divinity within. Seek that, and you will find what is real."

Ivaan sat quietly. The mountains, the sheep, the sky—all appeared unchanged. Yet within him, something had begun to shift. His heart was restless, like a compass trembling near magnetic truth. Though intellectually moved by his father's words, something in him still resisted total surrender. As if to steady himself, he turned the conversation—not to deny, but to inquire from another direction.

And in doing so, we return to the question that opened this journey. The same question that arose in a seeker's heart long ago: "By whose will and direction does the mind focus on its objects?"

On the surface, a thought arose in Ivaan's mind—subtle, fleeting, yet powerful enough to draw him inward. What gives birth to a thought? And by whose will does it arise?

From the standpoint of neuroscience, thoughts are the result of complex neural interactions—electrical impulses and chemical messengers dancing through the intricate circuits of the brain. These patterns are shaped by memory, experience, emotion, and environment. According to this view, Ivaan's thought was triggered by a stimulus—a word spoken, a feeling stirred, a memory recollected. It was, in essence, the brain responding to its surroundings.

Yet, even science finds itself at a boundary it cannot cross. It can trace the trajectory of thought, but not its origin. It can measure the firing of neurons, but not the spark that sets them alight. What chooses which neuron fires? What observes the thought arising?

Now consider this question through the lens of *Advaita Vedanta*.

Here, thoughts are not mere electrical surges—they are ripples in the lake of the mind, which itself is illumined by pure consciousness. According to *Vedanta*, Ivaan is not the creator of the thought, but the witness to the mind in which the thought appears. The mind is an instrument. The Self—the eternal, formless awareness—is the one who sees. It neither acts nor reacts. It simply is.

In this view, the thought does not "come" from somewhere. It arises within the field of consciousness, like a bird appearing against the vast sky. And in that moment, Ivaan's inquiry becomes more than intellectual curiosity—it becomes a soft awakening. A whisper from the eternal Self, calling him gently home.

This was no contradiction between science and spirituality—it was an invitation. One revealed the mechanism of thought, the other its mystery. And in the stillness between the two—in the silence between stimulus and response—the real answer began to glow. Perhaps the truest question was not 'What do we think?' but: 'Who is aware that we are thinking?'

In that moment, Ivaan sensed something stir—a presence deeper than thought, a ground beneath mind, memory, and even the fragile self he had always assumed himself to be. Consciousness was not an effect of the brain. It was the unmoving field in which all else appeared and disappeared.

The wind moved gently through the valley. A flock of sheep bleated in the distance. The silence between father and son grew thicker, no longer empty but pregnant with something unnamed. Ivaan felt as though he stood on the banks of a great uncharted river—not sure whether to step forward or retreat.

He turned to his father. Ayaan smiled, not with certainty but with peace—the kind of peace that comes not from knowing all the answers, but from asking the questions that truly matter.

And so, the journey had only just begun.

4
The Mirror of Love

The valley still echoed yesterday's silent questions. Ivaan moved along the familiar path, though each step now felt a little heavier with awareness, a little lighter with possibility. Born with the brilliance of a quiet flame, he carried a deep thirst for meaning. Seasons of solitude and observation had honed his spirit to a sharp edge. The shepherd's life, simple on the surface, had forged a quiet dignity within him. The winds taught him patience. The sheep shaped his silence. The mountains echoed his unspoken questions. His gaze had grown clearer; his will, more anchored. He moved like a seeker. Yet, in his stillness, he had begun to think like a sage.

Then came the off-season—a time when the pastures thinned, and the flock had to be returned. The mountains exhaled their first cold breath. The fields, once green and echoing with bells, now whispered about endings. As life often does in unseen ways, the universe turned a page in Ivaan's story.

That morning, the sun spilled its earliest light over the sleeping valley, casting a golden hush over the land. Everything stood in a kind of sacred stillness—as if the world itself were holding its breath for something unnamed but significant. Ivaan was on his way to return the sheep to the peasant he had borrowed them from.

Over the passing seasons, Ivaan and the flock had woven into an invisible bond. Through wind, rain, and still skies, they had become companions in silence. He had come to understand them not through words, but through rhythm, breath, and intuition. In their eyes, he discovered something ancient—something that watched without judgment and listened without needing answers.

Now, as if sensing the farewell, the sheep clustered around him. Their eyes held a softness that was beyond instinct—an awareness that seemed to recognize him. They brushed against him gently, as though in silent prayer. He knelt, running a hand over their coarse wool, whispering, "Until the snows melt, my friends… until we meet again."

His words floated into the valley, fragile as breath, anchored in love. The first full light of day fell over them—a quiet witness to a departure only the soul could feel.

The walk to the peasant's cottage was long and quiet. By the time he arrived, the sun had climbed above the hills. The man stood waiting, his eyes narrowing with habit, then widening in gentle surprise as he scanned the flock. They were strong, clean, cared for—each animal a testament to Ivaan's devotion.

A small smile tugged at the peasant's lips. He handed Ivaan his due—slightly more than he expected. Ivaan bowed in silent thanks, speaking only in thought: Good wool brings a fair price. Or perhaps the peasant saw more than fleece.

Yet, as he walked away, it was not wealth that filled him. The true reward was invisible: the companionship of animals, the hush of wind through the pines, the soft pulse of life in every leaf and stone. Something had shifted within him, quietly and unannounced—a whisper that life itself was more than a path trodden, that every step carried a secret lesson.

By late afternoon, the sky melted into amber and rose. The mountains glowed in shifting patterns of shadow and light. Ivaan moved slowly along the curved path, each step touching the earth with awareness. Wildflowers brushed his fingers; the river hummed a steady tune; the mountains held him in their embrace. A soft thought arose, as if the air itself had spoken: All that you seek is already within you, yet the heart must learn to see.

Then, as the path curved west and the breeze changed, she appeared.

He stopped. For a moment, he wondered if the sun had shaped her from its own light. She moved with the ease of the valley itself—slowly, quietly, rhythmically. Even the birds seemed to hush, and the wind stilled. In her eyes was a recognition older than memory—silent, profound, as if saying: 'I know you as the soul knows itself'.

She walked as if the earth itself breathed with her. Her pale pheran flowed like morning mist, carrying the quiet grace of the valley. Each step was measured, gentle—echoing a rhythm that felt older than time. Her presence seemed woven from silence and light, as though nature itself had lent her its harmony.

Her hair fell in loose waves, catching the sun in strands of shadow and gold, framing a face that held both tenderness and quiet strength. In her eyes was a depth that stilled the world—clear, calm, and infinite, like rivers meeting the sky. Her smile carried a quiet knowing—truths too vast for words, yet simple enough for the heart to feel.

Her eyes—deep, clear, endless—pulled him in, holding both rivers and skies. He felt something ancient stir within himself, as if the mountains themselves had been waiting to teach him this lesson: some presences arrive not by chance, but to awaken what has always been there.

She was not merely a woman; she was a living rhythm, a harmony of light and motion, a reflection of the valley, of the wind, of the sun. Every glance, every sway, spoke in a language older than time itself. And in that spell, Ivaan felt the tug of something eternal, something beautiful yet untouchable.

When she looked at him, the world fell away. Trees, hills, even the sun—all blurred into a shadow. In her gaze, he felt seen completely, without judgment, without effort. A question he had never dared to ask had already been answered.

And the valley whispered: love does not struggle. It flows. It arrives when the heart is ready, when the universe has woven its threads across lifetimes and suns. Recognition, not possession; presence, not need. Some meetings are not accidents. They are the returning of what was always meant to be.

"Are you a shepherd?" she asked, her voice gentle and clear—like the first drops of monsoon rain.

"I… I am," Ivaan said, voice catching, his throat suddenly dry. He cleared it, trying to steady himself under the weight of her presence. "And you are…?"

"Saira," she replied, her voice soft, warm and musical, like the memory of a familiar song. "I live nearby. I was picking flowers for my mother."

The name landed in him like the final note of a melody long forgotten. He studied her shy smile, the ease in her gestures, the quiet strength that seemed part of the valley itself. They fell into silence—not awkward, but full, like the space before a bell rings in a deserted temple, heavy with possibility.

"Would you walk with me?" she asked, her voice soft, carrying the warmth of sunlight on still water.

"Yes," he said—too quickly, too honestly. His feet moved before thought could catch up. At first stiff, he slowly eased into the rhythm she carried.

They walked beneath a canopy of golden chinar leaves, each leaf drifting down like a silent blessing. The valley itself seemed to lend its ears, holding its breath, as if the world recognized this meeting.

Saira spoke of simple things—the wild flowers that grew stubbornly between stones, her mother's small garden, the quiet joy of tending life in hidden corners—and of distant dreams, of snowy peaks that hid stories yet to be told. Her words were soft, but her presence carried a clarity that cut through thought. Some meetings need no reason; some hearts recognize each other before thought can comprehend.

Ivaan listened—not only to her words, but to the spaces between them. The gentle laughter that rose like temple bells. The way she brushed a strand of hair aside. The pauses that breathed life into everything she said. In that quiet, he felt the same presence he had felt with the mountains, the flock, the rhythm of wind and river; it was just that it now appeared in human form. The soul recognizes its own echo, he thought, even as words failed him.

It was not desire he felt, nor the urgent stirring of infatuation. It was recognition—an echo of something older than memory. A seed in the silent soil of his soul had stirred, awakened by a presence that needed no explanation. Love, he realized, could arrive not as distraction or passion, but as subtle awareness—a mirror of the self, reflected through another.

They reached a small clearing where the last light of day fell gently on the earth. Saira paused, turning to face him, half in light, half in shadow. The hush of the evening wrapped around them like a prayer. In that quiet, Ivaan sensed the invisible thread connecting them—a delicate, unspoken recognition, as if their souls had once danced together in some forgotten sky.

He instantly understood that the universe did not always speak through storms or revelations. Sometimes, it sent another soul to awaken what had always been present. The heart, when ready, recognizes itself in the stillness of another being.

"This is where I turn back," Saira said softly, her voice blending with the hush of the evening.

Ivaan hesitated, afraid that even a breath might push her further away. "Will I see you again?" he asked, though he already sensed the answer would not come in certainty.

Her eyes held a quiet promise, veiled in mystery. "Perhaps. If you walk this path again."

With deliberate steps, she began to recede, her presence gently fading into the twilight. The fragrance of wild flowers lingered, subtle and elusive, like a memory the mind refused to let go. Ivaan stood still, not from longing alone, but from a quiet awe—aware that some meetings are not meant to be clutched, but honoured.

The valley remained unchanged: the trees swayed, the breeze whispered, and life hummed on. Yet within Ivaan, something had shifted. The road ahead looked the same, but it carried the echo of something vast, invisible, unmistakable. His chest ached—not with sorrow, but with the quiet awareness of something sacred awakened.

He thought of her voice, her smile, the effortless rhythm of her steps, and understood that love is not merely attachment or desire. It is the language of the soul, spoken at a place where logic cannot reach. Even the sharpest mind, trained in silence, falters before *Maya*—not mere illusion, but the subtle force of recognition, when awakened hearts meet.

He sat on a rock as gold melted into indigo. Stars blinked awake, ancient witnesses to a truth felt but rarely spoken. In Saira's eyes, he glimpsed the invisible threads that bind the heart to the universe—the pulse of recognition, the beginning of meaning, the gentle power of awakening. Some encounters are not for possession, but for reverence. Some souls appear not to answer, but to awaken the questions that have always lived in silence.

5

The Threshold of Noise

Sometimes, stillness grows so full it begins to speak. And when it does, the seeker must listen—not with the ears, but with the heart.

Winter winds drifted down through the Kashmir valleys, sounding like whispers between chinar leaves, into homes and dreams. The land had changed. Fields once alive with bells and bleating now lay wrapped in mud and silence. The season of stillness had arrived.

Ivaan had returned the sheep to their owner. Days once shaped by rhythm and duty now stretched like unrolled parchment—blank, waiting. Winters had always been lean, Yet this year felt different. Not heavier, but charged, as if an unseen current moved beneath the ice.

A restlessness stirred within him. It wasn't the cold or the silence that unsettled him, but something deeper—a voice rising from within. Since meeting Saira, something in him had shifted. Her presence lingered like a half-remembered poem, a dream refusing to fade.

He could not explain it, but he knew with quiet certainty: it was time to leave. There was no fear—only a stoic realisation. The city called—not with noise, but with possibility. Delhi, distant and sprawling, beckoned him. He would go. Work if he must. Let winter pass. And come spring, he would return—to the mountains, to the sheep, and perhaps… to Saira.

That evening, by the hearth's crackle, he announced his decision. His voice surprised him with its steadiness. Ayaan said nothing at first. The thought of his only son leaving home pressed against his chest like snow against glass. Yet in Ivaan's eyes burned a calm, unwavering flame.

He had always known his son was not meant to remain bound to these hills. Some souls are born to outgrow the landscapes of their birth.

Ayaan nodded slowly. “Go,” he said, his voice low, tender. “See the world, my son. The mountains… will wait.”

Ivaan packed lightly, though his heart carried more weight than his satchel. At the doorway, Ayaan waited—face weathered, eyes steady, pride and worry rising like twin tides beneath them. He placed a hand on Ivaan’s head, fingers lingering as if pressing blessing into bone.

“Remember,” Ayaan whispered, “the mountains do not leave you when you leave them. Their silence walks with you.”

Ivaan bowed his forehead against his father’s hand. Words would have only fractured the moment.

Then he turned to the road. Behind him, the house still breathed of firewood, evening prayers, and questions never fully answered. With each step, the air thinned—as though part of him remained at the threshold.

The road curled into the valley like a line drawn by an unseen hand. Smoke from the hearth rose behind him, carrying pine and ash. Each step was double-edged: freedom in one foot, the ache of parting in the other.

The mountains did not call after him; they only watched—silent, eternal. Their stillness pressed at his back, not as farewell, but as witness.

Ahead lay distance, noise, the pulse of a world unknown. Yet beneath his unease ran a quiet certainty: this path was not chosen today—it had been written for him long before his feet touched the earth.

By twilight, he reached the station—a small island of clamour against the valley’s fading hush. Vendors cried, kettles hissed, children tugged at shawls, porters shouted animatedly.

Ivaan paused, absorbing it all. After seasons of wind and sheep-bells, this world struck him as violent—yet alive. And in that instant, he understood how deeply silence had shaped him.

The whistle rose in the distance—a long, trembling cry that split the valley. Ivaan turned toward the sound, heart unsteady but alive. For the first time, he felt not only that he was leaving, but that something within him was being called forward.

The train thundered in, iron grinding against iron, sparks tearing the quiet apart. Smoke billowed, acrid with coal. The crowd surged—bodies pressing, voices colliding, footsteps striking wood and stone like a relentless drumbeat.

Ivaan hesitated at the edge of the platform. For a breath, he thought of turning back—back to the hearth, the sheep, the gaze of the mountains, to Saira. But something steadier than fear rose in him, and he stepped into the current.

He found a seat by the window, clutching his satchel. The whistle pierced the air, and with a lurch, the train pressed forward.

The platform slid away. Faces blurred into shadows, lamps into faint streaks of light. The valley folded itself back into silence. Behind the smoke, the mountains loomed still—immovable witnesses, watching him leave.

Ivaan pressed his forehead against the glass. The wheels clattered—loud, insistent, unrelenting. Yet beneath the din, he felt a quieter hum, a silence carried like an ember within.

He closed his eyes. Leaving was not escape—it was continuation. Stillness had given its gift; now he would walk into the noise, carrying the question of who he was—not as burden, but as flame.

The train gathered speed. Night opened wide. And Ivaan, the seeker, crossed his first threshold into the unknown.

The train to Delhi would carry him from the hush of mountains to the roar of the capital. He didn't know what awaited him there—but he trusted the pull within. He wasn't running away. He was listening.

To something greater than comfort. To the language of the universe. To the call of his own being.

The journey stretched long, winding through shifting landscapes—snow-capped ridges fading into plains, crowded junctions, and the blur of nameless lives along the tracks. Each mile carried him farther from the familiar, yet closer to something stirring within.

At a small, nondescript station, the train halted, waiting for the signal. Restless, Ivaan stepped down. The platform was calm, dreamlike. Then, across the tracks, a superfast train roared in—passengers alighting, others rushing aboard. Moments later, it was gone.

A local train followed—noise, voices, hurried movement—then it too departed. Last came a goods train, crawling heavy and slow. No one boarded, no one disembarked. It sat in silence, then rolled away.

Ivaan watched quietly. A thought stirred: perhaps his own journey could not begin until these others had passed. Each train with its own rhythm, its own urgency.

And then he saw it.

It was not about the trains. It was about the station master.

The one who stood still while everything moved. Who watched, allowed, guided—yet never boarded a single train. He did not rush. He did not resist. He simply let movement pass through stillness.

A small moment. Easy to miss. But for Ivaan, it opened something vast.

As his train pulled forward again, the countryside blurring past, a quiet question rose within—older than his body, deeper than thought.

Since childhood, he had lived through countless moments—joy and sorrow, play and study, gain and loss. Friends came and went. Laughter rose and faded. No moment endured. Each was like a train: arriving, pausing and then vanishing into distance.

He thought of the infant once cradled in his mother's arms. The boy who ran barefoot through meadows. The teenager bent over books. And now—the young man gazing into a future he could not yet see.

All of these selves had passed like seasons. Yet, something remained.

Wasn't there someone within who had seen it all unfold? Like the station master—still, watchful—wasn't there a quiet witness inside him? One untouched by change, who observed joys and sorrows without clinging or fleeing?

A presence, constant and silent, behind the noise.

He closed his eyes, listening to the hum of wheels beneath him. The answer, he sensed, would never be found in thought—but only in silence. And for the first time, in the noise of a moving train, he felt truly still.

Who is the witness? Not the body—it shifts with time. Not the mind—its thoughts flicker like candle flames. Not the emotions—they rise and fall like waves. Then who?

He did not know. Yet the question itself was like a lamp lit in a dark room.

Wisdom rarely enters with thunder. It arrives like this—in whispers, in pauses most overlook. The world is noisy, entangled in desire. We live outwardly, reactively, missing what life keeps offering quietly. Apples had fallen for centuries before Newton looked up and saw. So too do ordinary events hold extraordinary truth—if one is ready.

The universe, he thought, does not reveal itself to the distracted. It speaks only to those inwardly still. Perhaps that is what separates the wise from the restless: the ability to witness without grasping, to be still amid motion.

In that moment, he saw himself reflected in the station master—one who stands present, watching, allowing. Not to escape life, but to live it more meaningfully. Perhaps that was why his train had been delayed. Perhaps the universe had paused him here—to learn, not by lecture, but by metaphor.

By the time the evening sky softened to dusky blue, the train paused at a small station. Passengers shuffled in and out. Among them was a man with a trimmed beard and steady eyes, who slipped quietly into the seat beside Ivaan. His clothes were plain, but chosen with care—as if tidiness was not a habit but an inner discipline.

As often happens on long journeys, a thread of conversation began. Most such exchanges vanish as quickly as they appear, names forgotten with the station. But now and then, a stranger becomes more—a mirror, a guide, even a messenger.

For Ivaan, this was such a moment.

"Are you living in Delhi?" the man asked, his voice calm, unhurried.

"No," Ivaan said. "I'm from Kashmir. I'm going to find part-time work. Winter is a lean season for shepherds."

The words carried no polish, no calculation. He spoke as one shaped by wind and stone, by silences deeper than words. Truth, for him, was not performance; it was breath, like the mountain air he had grown up with: sharp, unfiltered, alive.

That openness carried a quiet strength. He did not seek to impress. Yet, his presence invited trust. Even in his stillness, he seemed to answer questions not asked aloud.

The man smiled, eyes warm. "People call me *Sharma Ji*. I run a tea stall on the edge of Delhi. Nothing grand—just warmth in a cup, and a little kindness for whoever stops."

He paused, as though turning over something precious. "I come from Uttarakhand—where rivers are born, where silence between peaks teaches you how to listen. That silence shaped me. I have never chased wealth or fame. My only ambition is to remember the divine in every breath, and to serve whoever stands before me."

There was no pride in his tone—only peace. A man not driven by noise, but guided by stillness within.

"By His grace," he added softly, "life flows—sometimes swift, sometimes slow—but always with meaning. My family is content. I am content."

Then *Sharma Ji* turned gently toward him, eyes carrying the calm of an elder who has seen many storms and no longer fears the sky.

"And you, young man—what's your name?"

Something shifted in Ivaan—subtly, like warmth spreading in a cold room. For the first time since leaving home, he felt at ease. No mask, no guard.

"My name is Ivaan," he said, a small smile touching his lips. "And… if you don't mind, I would be grateful for your guidance. I've come to Delhi in search of part-time work—just enough to carry me through the winter. If you can show me where to begin, I'll be thankful."

There was no embellishment, only sincerity. A quiet offering of trust.

Perhaps *Sharma Ji* had known it from the moment he entered the compartment. Life has its own design, and some meetings are written before they happen. In Ivaan, he saw not just hands willing to work, but a spirit unspoiled—someone who could walk through the world without losing the truth of who he was.

Without hesitation, *Sharma Ji* nodded. "You can help me at the stall. It isn't much, but it's steady. Maybe that's what life is offering you, for now."

For a long second, Ivaan said nothing. Gratitude rose in him like a tide—wide, wordless, luminous. Was this what grace looked like? Each step of his journey had unfolded not with struggle, but with quiet ease—as though unseen hands were guiding him.

His leaving, the delay, this meeting—all had flowed like a current beneath the surface of things. Life was not just happening to him. It was happening for him.

And for the first time, he truly believed: Perhaps the universe does have a plan. Perhaps I am beginning to walk in it.

That night, they shared his dinner with *Sharma Ji* without fuss. When the compartment dimmed, Ivaan lay back on his berth, staring at the ceiling, listening to the hum of the train beneath him. Below, *Sharma Ji*'s breath moved with the sway of the wheels. Between them, there was no awkwardness, only peace—like two rivers that had quietly met.

They both knew: tomorrow would bring something new.

Morning arrived slowly. A pale light crept into the carriage as the train neared Delhi. Outside, a haze clung to the waking city. Fields had vanished into factories, forests into concrete. Silence dissolved into horns, footsteps, vendors shouting greetings. The capital was rising from sleep.

Ivaan sat upright, watching the world unfurl. Tangled wires webbed the sky like restless veins. Shops pressed against slums, hoardings screamed in clashing fonts. This was no Kashmir. Yet in his chest there was no fear—only wonder.

Beside him, *Sharma Ji* sipped from a steel flask, eyes steady, as though he had seen this chaos a thousand times and still bowed to its rhythm.

"Welcome to Delhi," he said, as the train gave its final shudder and slowed toward the platform.

Ivaan took a deep breath. The air smelled not of pine and snow, but of smoke and stories. He didn't know what awaited him beyond the gates. But something within was ready.

He smiled—softly, surely. The seeker had arrived.

PART TWO

Cosmic Conversations: Dialogue with the Universe

6

The Wisdom Cafe

The hiss of boiling milk, the clang of glass tumblers, the sharp smell of cardamom—this was Ivaan's new symphony. Within days, the tea stall became his world.

He rose with the shutters, wiped the counters, served steaming cups to men rushing to offices and rickshaw pullers wiping sweat from their brows. The work was simple: pour, serve, clean, repeat. Yet to Ivaan, it was never *just* work.

Every gesture mattered—the swirl of the spoon, the steady hand on the kettle, the way he looked a stranger in the eye when passing a cup. He believed even the smallest act could turn sacred if done with love and sincerity. *Anything less than a hundred percent,* he often told himself, *is a waste of life.*

This wisdom hadn't come from scriptures or lectures. It was carved into him by the mountains—the steely patience of grazing sheep, the rhythm of snow melting into streams, the silence that leaves no room for ego. Pride added nothing to a task. Humility took nothing away.

He gave the tea stall the same devotion another man might give a corner office. Every surface was scrubbed until it shone. Shelves were rearranged into proper order. He even suggested small but thoughtful changes to *Sharma Ji*—introducing clay cups instead of plastic, offering simple, nature-friendly snacks.

Soon, the shift was visible. Office workers paused on their way to meetings, students lingered after classes, morning joggers stopped for a refill.

They came for the tea, yes—but they stayed for something harder to name. There was a calm in the air, a stillness hidden beneath the bustle. Ivaan's presence seemed to weave it into every corner of the stall.

The earnings grew, but that was not the real gain. What touched *Sharma Ji* was watching the boy at work. Ivaan did not serve for profit, nor even for gratitude. He moved with reverence—as if each cup poured was a prayer. In a city that thrived on urgency, here was someone unhurried, anchored, already at home.

Perhaps the universe places such souls on purpose—not to turn the whole world overnight, but to spread light in small corners, one humble act at a time.

Life quickened. The stall, more vibrant than ever, demanded constant attention. From dawn to late evening, the two men moved in rhythm—serving, refilling, cleaning, counting. Their conversations shrank to quick exchanges about supplies or customers. Words became fewer, but the silence between them carried an ease. The days passed like water—swiftly, softly and unnoticed.

Then, one afternoon, the city shifted its mood. A sudden spell of winter rain swept across Delhi, soft but steady, washing the dust from the air. The morning's clear sky folded into a muted grey. Streets that had roared with traffic on other days now lay hushed, puddles gathering in their cracks, neon signs reflected in the water like wavering dreams.

Around the tea stall, the usual rush thinned into stillness. For the first time in many days, there was a lull.

Customers came in only now and then. And so the two men simply sat, listening to the rain drumming on the tin roof. Ivaan boiled water, added slivers of ginger, and poured two steaming cups. He offered one to *Sharma Ji* with a quiet smile. Without a word, *Sharma Ji* took it and lowered himself onto the wooden bench beside him.

For a while, neither of them spoke. The rain seemed enough.

At last, *Sharma Ji* broke the silence. He raised his cup, breathing in the rising steam. "This rain," he murmured, "reminds me of the hills. Back home, when the forests drank rainwater, the whole valley smelled like prayer."

Ivaan's eyes softened. "In Kashmir too, rain in winter carries a promise. It whispers that snow is not far behind."

Their smiles met across the silence, two men held together by memory—of landscapes gentler than this city, of lives measured not by hurry, but by seasons.

It was in that silence, sheltered by the rain, that their stories began to surface—not in grand declarations, but gently, like ripples widening on a still pond.

Sharma Ji spoke first, recalling the mornings of his youth in Uttarakhand, when temple bells broke the dawn and tea was offered not as commerce but as prayer. His voice softened as memory carried him back to valleys where devotion was woven into daily life.

Ivaan, in turn, shared the rhythms of Kashmir—the sheep he once herded across meadows, the long winters when silence itself seemed alive, and the unseen presence that had always guided him, quiet but all-encompassing.

It became clear then: theirs was not a bond of mere labour. Something deeper moved beneath the surface—two seekers crossing paths, not by accident, but by a hidden orchestration. The rain did not halt the world; it simply slowed their corner of it long enough for truth to emerge.

Sometimes, it takes no grand upheaval to alter a life's course. A quiet afternoon, two cups of tea, and a passing rain can be enough—when the soul is ready.

Sharma Ji's gaze lingered on the curtain of drizzle beyond the stall. His words came out unhurried, carrying the weight of years, not as burden but as clarity.

"You know why I worship here, day after day, and again at home?" he asked. He did not wait for Ivaan's reply.

"It is this: if you worship with a true heart, God will never leave you to walk alone in this restless world. Worship does not erase suffering—it was never meant to. But it makes a promise: that when pain comes, you will not face it by yourself. God will walk beside you. I have seen it. I have felt it. Not once, but time and again."

He paused, turning to Ivaan with a softness only a father would do. "There's another secret I'll share with you, my son," he said, resting a hand on the boy's shoulder. The word *son* was not politeness, but sincerity. "You remind me of my own. And what I would tell him, I tell you now."

"Many people," *Sharma Ji* continued, "stand before idols as though they are lifeless stones. That is where they go astray. When you pray, prepare your mind—not to see stone, but to meet a Presence. Don't bow to an object. Bow to the living deity who sees you, hears you, and answers you in the language of your devotion."

Ivaan listened, the warmth of the tea fading in his palms, though a deeper warmth was kindling in his chest.

Sharma Ji's voice softened to a whisper. "And remember this—never pray as if God were a shopkeeper of blessings. Don't bargain. Don't plead. If you truly felt the deity before you, alive and present—could you dare to ask for something? No. You would fall silent, awestruck, humbled. Only when people secretly doubt the deity's presence do they demand endlessly. It is easier to ask from stone than from the Living."

He drew a steady breath; eyes glistening, yet calm. "When your heart knows, when your mind is fixed in the truth, you see it—God is not locked in a shrine. The whole world becomes divine. Every face, every struggle, every fleeting moment—He lives in them all."

A gentle smile touched his lips, as if he were remembering something ancient and true. "And one more thing, Ivaan," he said, turning his cup slowly between his hands. "Just as we leave our shoes outside before stepping into a temple, so too must we leave our expectations at the threshold of the Divine. Only then does worship become real."

He paused for a moment, letting the weight of his words settle in.

"Because when we carry desires into prayer," *Sharma Ji* said softly, "we are not really meeting God—we are only meeting our own reflections, our own wants. True prayer begins when the asking ends. When you can stand before the deity with nothing to beg for, nothing to demand—only a quiet offering of your presence—that is when you are truly in the temple. That is when He truly sees you."

The words sank into Ivaan like rain drops into dry earth. Something sacred was being carved silently into the walls of his mind. The lesson was simple yet immense: prayer was not about ritual but surrender. Not about wishes fulfilled, but about the complete absence of wishes, ready to be filled with something higher.

"Leave your shoes," *Sharma Ji* repeated with a serene smile, "but more importantly, leave your expectations. That is the first real step inside."

Silence followed—yet it was not empty. It was full: of grace, of understanding, of a bond forming between seeker and guide, between a boy and the father the universe had chosen for his journey. The rain outside had ceased; but within, a deeper current had begun to flow.

In India, tea stalls have always carried such currents. They are far more than places for a hot drink. They are the quiet cafés of wisdom scattered across the land, standing at crossroads and markets, outside bus stops and offices—humble counters that witness humanity in motion. Here, over clay cups, strangers and friends alike pause to debate, to question, to dream.

At one stall, a cricket match is relived ball by ball. At another, politics is argued with the fervour of parliament. Elsewhere, voices wander into philosophy and science—why the mind cannot grasp the full universe, whether the soul exists beyond reason, whether truth belongs to sages or to seekers. From the fate of nations to the meaning of life, all pass through the steam of boiling tea.

And during election seasons, the stalls transformed into centres of ground-level wisdom. The voices here belonged not to analysts with charts or anchors with agendas, but to ordinary men and women whose intuition has been sharpened by life itself. Their predictions often matched—sometimes even surpassed—the precision of scientific polls, for they observed people closely, listened deeply, and spoke without masks.

For Ivaan, this world was both chaotic and captivating. The stall was noisy, cluttered, alive—but also full of raw, unpolished truths. He rarely joined the debates unless asked. Instead, he listened—not lazily, but with an alert stillness. He discovered there is an intelligence in listening without rushing to reply, in simply witnessing. Like the station master he had once observed, he began to cultivate the role of a silent observer.

Some conversations amused him, others tested his patience, and a few struck chords that lingered long after the crowd dispersed. Yet he learned not to take in everything. Slowly, he began to filter noise from wisdom, emotion from insight, chatter from clarity.

In this little corner of Delhi, Ivaan was no longer just serving tea. He was absorbing life. The stall had become his school, the customers his teachers, the conversations his lessons. And perhaps, in truth, it was never tea that was being served here at all—it was awareness, reflection, and the human experience, poured out one cup at a time.

One afternoon, three elderly men gathered at the stall, their faces lined not only with age but with thought. Two of them, both with distinguished beards and clipped accents, hailed from the United Kingdom. The third was an Indian philosopher. From their manner, it was clear they had come to Delhi for a prestigious science conference. Yet their conversation betrayed a quiet dissatisfaction, as if the grandeur of the event had left some deeper question unanswered.

As steam curled upward from their cups, their words stretched across the vast distances between physics and philosophy. They spoke of the elusive *Theory of Everything*—the ultimate framework that might bind together all the laws of the cosmos. But woven into their voices was a note of frustration. The unification they sought always appeared just beyond reach.

Dr. Simon Daniel, one of Britain's leading physicists, tapped his cup for emphasis. "The Theory of Everything is no fantasy," he insisted. "Hawking showed us that black holes obey quantum principles. Einstein spent his final years in search of the answer. Now, with string theory, we stand closer than ever. Imagine it—a single equation to explain every force, every particle, every law of nature!"

The Indian philosopher, Dr. Arvind Iyer, lifted his cup with quiet grace before replying. His words shifted the ground beneath the discussion. "But what if this theory itself is an illusion? Perhaps the universe is not meant to be caged within human equations. Einstein failed. Even Hawking admitted that gravity and quantum mechanics may never fully merge. Why assume this quest has an end at all?"

Dr. Daniel leaned forward, eyes alight with the fire of conviction. "Failure in the past does not mean failure forever. The Higgs boson was once only theory—now it is fact. Science advances, step by step. Theory exists. We only need to uncover it."

The third man, Dr. Richard Holt, an astrophysicist from Cambridge, let out a weary sigh and placed his cup gently on the counter. "We are trapped in a paradox," he said. "General relativity explains the vast cosmos, quantum mechanics explains the microscopic world—but when we try to merge them, the mathematics collapses into singularities. The equations tear themselves apart."

He leaned back, eyes narrowed. "Einstein spent decades trying to unify gravity with electromagnetism, but he lacked the quantum tools we hold today. String theory claims that every particle is a vibrating strand, integrating gravity with elegance. But where is the proof? Eleven dimensions? Countless hidden universes? None of it can be tested."

Simon Daniel shook his head, his voice quickening with conviction. "They once said the same about black holes. For decades, they were nothing but mathematical ghosts—until we saw them. The fact that string theory even contains gravity in its framework is extraordinary. And it is not alone. Loop Quantum Gravity argues that space itself is not smooth but made of tiny, indivisible loops. Imagine—reality itself, pixelated!"

Dr. Arvind Iyer, the philosopher, raised a hand, his tone calm, almost gentle. "And yet, both theories remain unproven. Perhaps that is the point. Perhaps science will always remain incomplete, just as human beings can never fully measure the infinite. What if this yearning for a 'final theory' is itself an illusion?"

For a moment, silence reigned. Rainwater dripped from the awning into the street.

Then Simon Daniel spoke again, slower now, as though confessing to himself as much as others. "Maybe you are right. Maybe the universe resists simplification. But history also teaches us this—every time we thought the horizon of knowledge was fixed, we found it was only the beginning. Newton thought gravity absolute—Einstein shattered that. Einstein thought the cosmos static—then Hubble proved it was expanding. Hawking once swore black holes destroyed information—later he recanted. The only constant in science is that we keep moving forward."

The philosopher's smile carried both gentleness and certainty. "And yet," Dr. Iyer said, "perhaps the ultimate truth is not in an equation at all, but in experiencing the universe as it is—without the compulsion to define or contain it."

Their discussion resolved nothing, and perhaps that was its raison d'etre. The universe did not wish to be concluded; it wished to remain an open question, an endless mystery inviting exploration.

The tea stall was strangely quiet. Delhi stalls were rarely deserted. Yet the benches stood empty today, the usual chorus of chatter and clinking glasses conspicuous by their absence. Only the three distinguished men remained, their words curling into the still air.

Ivaan noticed this odd hush but did not question it. Whatever the reason, it gave him a rare gift: the chance to overhear a conversation unlike anything he had known.

The language was dense—physics, philosophy, strange names and theories—but he caught the essence. He was not highly schooled. Yet, his curiosity was sharper than most. He understood not the details, but the hunger in their voices: the human longing to grasp the ultimate.

He listened with a still intensity, his hands moving mechanically through the chores of wiping cups and rearranging jars. Inside, however, he was aflame. He longed to speak, to ask, to test his own small questions against their great ones. But hesitation chained his tongue. What right did a tea boy have to interrupt such minds?

Just as courage was stirring within him, the two physicists rose. A few final words were exchanged, a nod, a glance at the time—and then they were gone. Their departure left only Dr. Arvind Iyer at the table, staring into the dregs of his tea, lost in thought.

Dr. Iyer ordered another cup of tea and sat in silence, his gaze turned inward, lost in the depths of thought.

Ivaan's heart pounded. This was his moment. He had always believed that an Indian thinker might be more approachable than the foreign scientists, more likely to listen. If he didn't try now, the chance would slip away forever.

He drew a deep breath and stepped forward, positioning himself quietly beside Dr. Iyer. Hands clasped, back straight, he waited with the patience of a disciple before a teacher.

Slowly, Dr. Iyer returned from his reverie. His eyes blinked back into focus, settling on the young boy who had served him tea.

"Would you clean the table?" Dr. Iyer asked casually.

Ivaan shook his head gently. "No, sir. You can remain seated. If you wish, I can bring you another cup of special tea."

The philosopher smiled faintly. "No, thank you. I should be leaving soon. Tell me, how much do I owe you?"

Ivaan hesitated, his breath catching in his throat. Then, with a courage that surprised even himself, he spoke. "I will tell you the price, sir… but may I ask you something first? A question that has been burning in me since I heard your discussion."

Dr. Iyer tilted his head, his curiosity awakened.

Ivaan's voice trembled at first, then steadied. "Is it truly possible to define the universe with one theory? To hold it all in a single idea? I don't know the mathematics, but I heard enough to feel the longing behind your words. If you believe I am worthy of even a little understanding, please… enlighten me."

For a moment, Dr. Iyer simply stared. The tea stall seemed to fade around them, as though the world itself had paused to listen. In the boy's eyes he saw no arrogance, no pretension—only a rare purity: eagerness, humility, and a thirst for truth untarnished by ego.

Something stirred in the philosopher's chest, a recognition beyond reason. This was no ordinary tea boy.

Softly, he asked, "Where are you from?"

Ivaan straightened, his voice steady yet gentle. "I am a shepherd from Kashmir. This is the lean season—there is little scope to graze the sheep in the valley. So, I came here, to work and support my family."

His words carried no complaint, only resilience. And it was this simplicity that touched Dr. Arvind Iyer. For the first time in a long while, he felt not the weight of argument, but the presence of sincerity.

Leaning forward, his tone softened, but his eyes gleamed with an ancient light. "Yes," he said, "there is a theory that defines the universe. But it is not written in physics, nor hidden in equations. It is a truth older than science, older than language itself."

He let the silence hang, watching the boy's anticipation.

"Let me show you with something simple. Imagine a potter shaping pots—some large, some small, some plain, some ornate. To the eye, they are all different. But in truth, each is nothing but clay in form. The shapes may change, but the essence remains the same. If you understand the clay, you understand every pot that will ever be made."

Ivaan's breath caught. The analogy settled into him like a seed into fertile soil. He realized he had always looked at the "pots"—the sheep, the mountains, the people, even himself—yet rarely had he thought about the "clay" that lay beneath them all.

He nodded slowly, not out of politeness, but because something inside him had just shifted.

"Now, consider gold," Dr. Iyer continued. "There are countless ornaments—rings, necklaces, bracelets, crowns. Each seems unique; yet at the core, they are nothing but gold. The ring may be small, the crown may be grand, but their essence does not change. If you know the gold, you already know every ornament. Without gold, none of them could exist at all."

He let the words linger, then drew the thread tighter.

"In the same way, everything you see—people, mountains, rivers, stars—is but form. Behind the forms lies one ultimate reality. We grow so attached to shapes and their differences that we forget the essence that holds them all together. That essence is eternal, unchanging truth."

Ivaan's eyes flickered with unease and wonder. "Does this mean," he asked softly, "that everything is just an illusion?"

Dr. Iyer's smile deepened. He looked at Ivaan approvingly. "Not illusion in the sense of nothingness, but illusion in the sense of misunderstanding. The pot is not other than the clay, the ring is not other than the gold. In the same way, you are not other than that ultimate reality. The world is real, but our way of perceiving it—as separate, divided, fragmented—that is the illusion. That illusion is called *Maya*. When you pierce through it, when you see the oneness behind all forms, the universe is revealed as it truly is."

The evening air hung still, as though holding its breath. Something shifted in Ivaan—not a final answer, but the first glimpse of a truth vast enough to change the course of his seeking.

Dr. Iyer studied the boy's glowing eyes, then leaned back slightly, pausing, as if weighing his next words.

"Many scientists," Dr. Iyer continued, "have already glimpsed this truth in flashes, though they often frame it in their own language. They strive for a single theory that will define the entire universe—what they call the 'Theory of Everything.' They believe that if it is ever found, it will explain the universe's birth, predict its end, decide whether we live in a single cosmos or countless multiverses, and unravel the deepest mysteries of existence."

He paused, his gaze steady.

"But I have my doubts. Science works within the realm of what can be observed and measured. The ultimate reality, however, lies beyond all perception, beyond the nets of time, space, and causation. Equations can describe forms and forces. But can they ever capture the essence that gives rise to them? Can the eternal be measured with the tools of the temporary?"

Ivaan's brows furrowed slightly, as though standing on the edge of a thought too vast to hold.

Dr. Iyer softened his tone. "Let me tell you a story. It may bring the idea closer."

He leaned forward, hands folded as if preparing to pass on something ancient.

"A group of ten men were traveling together. They came to a wide river, its current fierce. But they had no choice but to cross it. Somehow, with effort and fear, they reached the far shore. Exhausted, the leader decided to count everyone, just to be sure all had survived. He pointed at each man—one, two, three… nine. Alarmed, he said, 'One of us is missing!' Each one in the group in turn tried to count, and each arrived at nine. Panic spread: surely one had drowned."

Dr. Iyer looked at Ivaan, his eyes glinting. "Do you see the error already?"

A faint smile crossed Dr. Iyer's lips as he leaned back, letting the story breathe.

"You see, Ivaan," he said softly, "the tenth man was never missing. Only forgotten. In the same way, the essence of the universe—Consciousness itself—has never been absent. It is here, now, at the heart of every being. But we forget. We count the ornaments, the pots, the stars, the equations… and we miss the very Self that is doing the counting."

He paused, his gaze steady and compassionate.

"Scientists, philosophers, seekers—we are all like those ten men. Searching outside for what is never lost inside. The universe does not need to be defined—it needs to be *remembered*. And when you discover that you are not separate from that essence, the search ends in silence, not in formulas."

Ivaan felt a shiver move through him. The parable was simple, almost childlike, yet its truth pierced deeper than any learned argument. It was as if a veil had been pulled back, revealing not an answer, but a direction—toward himself.

The evening light had thinned into twilight. The tea stall glowed faintly under its single bulb, but for Ivaan, a brighter light had been kindled within.

"Perhaps science will come closer," Dr. Iyer said, "but can it ever step beyond its own limits? Can the mind—part of the illusion itself—ever grasp what lies beyond illusion? That is the real question."

Without pausing to consider whether the boy could follow, he went on, his voice calm yet weighted with years of contemplation, as though he were not teaching but unveiling something already present.

"The ultimate reality is nothing but pure Consciousness. You, Ivaan, are not merely flesh and bone. You are not even just energy. What makes you alive, aware, sentient—is Consciousness itself. It shines upon your mind, and the mind reflects it, like the moon reflecting sunlight. The mind then lights up your senses, and through them your body comes alive. And so you say, 'I am.'"

He paused, watching the boy carefully.

For Ivaan, the words felt less like an explanation and more like a mirror. He could almost sense it—that behind his thoughts, behind his breath, behind even his act of listening, there was something vast, silent, unchanging. Something that had always been there.

"Not only you, Ivaan—every living being is alive only because Consciousness reflects in the mind. That is the supreme truth. Yet in ignorance, we mistake ourselves for the body and mind. We cling to thoughts, emotions, identities, forgetting they are only fleeting waves rising and falling within the ocean of Consciousness. The one who awakens to this never again bows before illusion. For the one who knows this truth… knows everything."

Dr. Iyer's eyes deepened, his voice carrying both urgency and tenderness.

"But to make this knowledge a living reality is not easy. The mind is not prepared. For countless lifetimes, it has been trained to look outward—always seeking, always grasping. It commands the senses like a tyrant, sending them into the world to collect experiences. The senses obey, and the mind weaves these into memories, attachments, desires. Thus, it becomes tangled in its own net, never allowing itself to turn inward, never returning to the source from which it draws its light. Restless, it moves outward again and again—searching, but never finding."

He paused, letting the words settle like seeds.

For Ivaan, it was as if Dr. Iyer had placed a mirror before him—not of his face, but of his inner being. He could feel the truth of it, not as mere philosophy, but as a description of his own restless thoughts, his own seeking.

He leaned forward, his voice softening yet deepening, carrying a gravity that seemed to press against the edges of reality.

"Rare," he said, *"is the soul who trains the mind as a mahout tames a wild elephant, who restrains the senses as a tortoise withdraws its limbs at the first hint of danger. Through relentless discipline, through contemplation that pierces illusion, such a person begins to perceive the ultimate truth: they are not the body, not the mind, not even the individual self. They are nothing but pure, infinite Consciousness. And when this realisation dawns, there is nothing more to seek, nothing more to attain. That soul is fulfilled—they have merged with the eternal truth. They have become what they always were. Consciousness, in its entirety, is the Theory of Everything."*

A profound silence followed. Outside, the clamour of the tea stall—the clinking of cups, the hum of voices—faded into irrelevance. The air felt charged, as if the very fabric of existence had momentarily parted, allowing a glimpse of its boundless essence.

Ivaan, young and unversed in such mysteries, felt a stirring within him—a flicker of recognition, as if some long-forgotten truth had nudged him awake.

Without a word, without leaving any room for questions, Dr. Iyer rose. His movement was deliberate, final, as if the teaching had been complete in a single moment. From his pocket, he drew a large currency note and placed it gently into Ivaan's hand.

Ivaan looked up, startled—not by the money, but by the weight in Dr. Iyer's gaze.

"My boy," Dr. Iyer said, his voice both warm and unshakable, *"in your eyes, I see more than understanding. I see that you have felt the essence of my words, that you have absorbed them into your being. And beyond that, I see belief—pure, sincere belief. That is a rare flame, one that transforms knowledge into existence itself."*

He paused, studying the boy with a gaze that seemed to measure not just the surface, but the very depths of his being.

"I also sense," he said, *"within you the capacity to realize the ultimate truth—the Theory of Everything I spoke of. Your heart is simple, your mind unclouded, and your intellect sharp. These are the very qualities needed to perceive reality as it truly is. Only a little effort remains to transform this knowledge into direct realization—here and now, within this life."*

Dr. Iyer placed a steady hand on Ivaan's shoulder, his voice carrying the weight of an ancient certainty. *"Make your mind as pure as a superconductor—free from resistance, allowing truth to flow without hindrance. This is accomplished through right action, through Karma, and through unwavering devotion, through Bhakti. Purify the mind, and realization will arise on its own, like the dawn that inevitably follows the night."*

Without another word, Dr. Iyer turned and walked away, fading into the soft glow of the evening, leaving behind not just an empty teacup, but a profound and indelible mark upon the young boy's heart.

Ivaan stood frozen for a heartbeat, the currency note trembling in his hand. Yet his mind was far from such material concerns. A memory had been etched into the stillness of the tea stall—a memory that would grow, deepen, and perhaps, one day, transform the very fabric of his existence.

Then, as if awakened from a sacred trance, the stillness shattered. The tea stall, which had seemed a sanctuary of quiet, sprang back to life—chairs scraped, cups clinked, voices overlapped, and orders were shouted across the counter. The universe had resumed its familiar rhythm, indifferent to the extraordinary exchange that had just occurred.

Ivaan blinked, returning to the present. Duty called. He tucked the note safely into his pocket and resumed his tasks—serving tea, clearing tables, tending to the endless stream of customers. Yet even as his hands moved through the motions, his mind was elsewhere—turning, questioning, unravelling. Dr. Iyer's words did not fade into the background; they lingered, taking root, planting a seed deep within him.

Something had shifted.

And though the world around him continued its habitual cadence, Ivaan knew, with an unspoken certainty, that he could never see it the same way again.

7
The Silent Teacher

Ivaan awoke at 4 a.m. without hesitation. Rising early had never felt like a burden; it was as if dawn itself had been stitched into the fabric of his being since childhood. Outside, the city slept beneath a heavy quilt of fog. The air was sharp, biting against his skin even as he lingered under the blanket. Streetlights glimmered faintly through the mist—like reluctant stars that had lost their way.

He moved quietly to the kitchen, where the first ritual of the day awaited him. Boiling water, the slow unfurling of tea leaves, the curling ascent of steam—it was all a meditation disguised as routine. In this fragile hour, before the noise of the world intruded, Ivaan felt closest to something he could not name.

After the deep surrender of the night, he knew he had slept well. And yet, a question pressed upon him: *How did he know?* Sleep was a void. No memories lingered, no visions remained. It was as if his awareness had dissolved into nothingness. If that was so, who within him could testify to this rest?

The thought unsettled him. Perhaps it was simply the absence of fatigue that convinced him he had slept. But another possibility whispered: that some hidden part of him never truly slept. A witness, invisible and silent, remained awake when his mind had vanished. A presence beyond thought, beyond dream, beyond time itself.

If such a witness existed, what was it? Not Ivaan, the man who brewed tea, carried memories, and bore the weight of a name. No, this was something older, something that did not belong to him but to existence itself.

The realization both fascinated and disturbed him. Was he merely the echo of this witness, playing at being human while something eternal looked on? And if so, who was he really?

His thoughts swirled dangerously close to answers his mind could not contain—until the ordinary world reclaimed him. The fragrance of tea filled the room, dissolving the silence with its warmth. Dawn was breaking, and with it, another day.

Just then, a sound tore through the stillness: the low rumble of a lorry halting outside. From its shadow stepped a tall man. His beard, long and heavy, was damp with fog; a woollen blanket clung to his shoulders, and a worn turban crowned his head. He walked as though the earth itself yielded to his pace, unhurried, unbound.

"When the tea is ready, serve me a cup." The man's voice was calm, carrying the weight of centuries.

Ivaan observed the man carefully. Something in his presence resisted explanation. He had seen countless wanderers before—drivers, labourers, men who lived and died on the road. Yet this one carried himself differently. The fog clung to him as if reluctant to let him go, and time itself seemed to slow with his steps.

The tea was ready. Ivaan poured the first cup and placed it before the stranger. The street was still deserted; dawn had not yet broken through the fog. Today felt unlike other mornings. The man had arrived precisely as the tea was poured, as though drawn by an invisible hand, as though this meeting had been written long before either of them awoke.

The stranger lifted the cup, inhaled deeply, and drank. His eyes were not merely tired; they were weighted with the dust of endless journeys, the silence of miles uncounted. When he finally spoke, his voice seemed to rise not only from his throat, but from some cavern of memory.

"Those with uncluttered hearts," he said slowly, "draw the right souls into their orbit. The universe does not always explain itself, yet it never falters in arranging the encounters that shape us."

He paused, as if his own words tasted of both truth and sorrow.

"My name is Khushwant Singh. Amritsar is my home. For twenty-five years, I have driven lorries across this land, carrying goods, carrying silence. I have seen cities that never sleep and villages where time itself has forgotten to move. My work is simple, yes—but simplicity is deceptive. Beneath it lie days without end, nights under the naked sky, and an intimacy with roads that never promises return."

Ivaan wiped the counter with slow, deliberate strokes, unsettled by the intimacy of this confession. He had not asked for it. Why was this stranger, freshly emerged from fog, placing his life in Ivaan's hands as if it were a fragile offering? He was only a boy in a tea stall. What wisdom could he possibly mirror back to a man carved by roads and years?

At last, he asked, almost involuntarily, "Why are you telling me all this?"

The man's lips curved into a half-smile. "Because there is no real distance between you and me. Between boy and man, traveller and server, seeker and guide. We walk different roads, but the same sky witnesses us all."

Silence swelled between them, but it was not empty. It had the density of unspoken truth, the fullness of something both had felt but neither dared name.

"I do not usually stop for tea at this hour," Khushwant continued. "Yet today my heart tugged me here. The fog is thicker, the air carries a strange clarity. And when I saw you, the steam rising, the first cup poured—something within me knew this moment was chosen. Chosen not by me, nor by you, but by something larger."

He looked directly at Ivaan now, his gaze unwavering, kind yet piercing.

"You are young, burning with brightness. Why are you here, tethered to this stall?"

Ivaan hesitated. He did not wish to reveal his story, nor could he dishonor the stranger with a lie. He spoke little, just enough to sketch an outline.

Khushwant listened in silence, nodding as though he heard what Ivaan had withheld. Then, with a breath heavy as confession, he said:

"When I was nineteen, not older than you, I worked in a sugarcane factory. I had no grand plans for the future. Life seemed a straight corridor without windows. And then, in a single morning, that corridor collapsed. My father—also a lorry driver—died in an accident. The world lost its shape. I still remember the moment they told me. The air itself refused to move; time became a cruel statue. In that instant, I died for the first time—not in flesh, but in spirit."

He stopped, his eyes dark with remembrance.

"Fate was merciless. Within months, my mother too was gone. No illness was named, but grief is a disease more fatal than any. Her silence swallowed her, and I was left to wander a world suddenly stripped of shelter. There was no hand to steady me, no voice to remind me that meaning could return. People came, offered condolences, and went back to their lives. But their words rang hollow, their visits stank of duty or, worse, of curiosity. And I learned the hardest truth of all: suffering isolates more completely than distance ever could."

The fog outside thickened. Inside, the silence between them grew dense, like a third presence at the table.

"Then, one day," Khushwant continued, his voice lowering as if speaking across years, "a holy man from town came to see me. He was not a man of wealth or power, but people bowed before him, for his words carried the gravity of knowledge. He sat beside me, as if my grief belonged to him as well, and spoke words that at the time I could not grasp. They were like drops of rain falling on a parched earth—strange, almost foreign—but in time, they became the roots of my healing."

The stranger's eyes grew distant, as though recalling a moment that still burned inside him.

"He told me, *'Everything moves by reason, though your eyes may not see it. What you endure is not an exception but a law of life itself. Human beings weigh their sorrows by the scales of personal loss, forgetting that the universe measures differently. Your parents have left in form and name, and no matter how you weep or call, they will not return. Yet in their absence, something else is struggling to be born in you.'*

"Then he spoke of Gautama Buddha, and his words pierced me deeper than the wound of my grief. *'Imagine an arrow entering your flesh,'* he said. *'Its pain is sharp, undeniable. That is the first arrow—the blow of fate, the law of cause and effect, written long before you knew it. But the second arrow—ah, that is of your own making. It is your refusal, your resistance, your anger at what cannot be undone. One arrow is inevitable. The other is your choice. Remove it, and you begin to heal. Cling to it, and you bleed twice over.'*

"I remember sitting there, torn open by sorrow, yet a strange clarity touched me. His words did not bring my parents back. They did not erase the loneliness that howled inside me. But they carved a new space in my mind—a place where grief and understanding could sit together without devouring each other. For the first time since my world had shattered, I felt the faint stirrings of breath again."

Khushwant's hands trembled slightly as he gripped his cup.

"I gathered my courage and asked him, 'Tell me, Master, what should I do now? How must I live?'

"He looked at me with eyes that seemed to see through birth and death alike. His voice was not commanding, nor gentle—it was like the wind that moves whether you notice or not.

'Your lifespan is already written,' he said. *'Even if despair tempts you, you cannot die before your appointed hour. Life will hold you until the last breath is marked. But within that span, you alone must choose. You can live with awareness, or you can drown in confusion. The choice is yours, and no one else can make it for you.'*

"He told me of two paths.

'One is the path of renunciation. Leave behind the weight of desire, the chains of family, wealth, ambition. Walk as a monk, live as devotion itself. In surrender, the burden of suffering dissolves, and in time, the river of your soul returns to the ocean of God, where no grief can follow.'

But then his voice grew heavier.

"If you remain in the world, know this: suffering will not spare you. Desire will chase you endlessly, and each desire births attachment. What you love, you will one day lose. What you cling to, life will tear away from your hands. Joy will be real, yes—but so will sorrow, in equal measure. Unless you awaken, you will mistake this endless cycle for life itself.'

Khushwant fell silent, his words hanging like incense in the cold air. Ivaan felt as though he had been listening not to one man's past, but to a truth that belonged to all who dared to ask why they lived.

"The world itself," the holy man said, "is neither good nor bad. It is only a mirror. If you see suffering reflected in it, it is because sorrow already nests within you. If you see peace, it is because peace is alive within you. The question is not whether you choose the world or renounce it—the question is: *how will you walk the path that is yours?*"

His words struck me like a riddle. I longed to ask, *Can everyone who suffers become a monk? Can every wounded soul simply renounce the world?* But the question froze inside me. His presence was not loud, yet it pressed upon me with the weight of mountains. He spoke with the authority of one who had glimpsed life and death from the inside, and I feared that any challenge would shatter me before it ever touched him.

Still, doubt gnawed at me. Was escape the only answer? Was freedom possible only in deserts and monasteries, far from the pulse of the world? Couldn't a man remain in the marketplace, carrying both his grief and his humanity, and still transcend?

I remained silent. Perhaps it was fear. Perhaps reverence. Or perhaps, more truthfully, I was not ready to hear the answer, because hearing it would demand a choice I did not yet have the strength to make.

The holy man looked at me with eyes that seemed to know every unspoken thought. He did not argue, did not press. Wisdom does not force itself; it waits, like a seed waits for the season of rain. Without another word, he stood up and walked into the mist of morning, his figure dissolving into the fog until I could no longer tell whether he had ever been there at all.

But he left me with a silence that weighed heavier than speech. The choice between renunciation and the world was not a simple fork in the road—it was a fire in the chest, a question that would not leave me. Perhaps the real challenge was not to escape life, but to live it without being devoured by it.

Days bled into nights, and the ache within me did not lessen. Time did not heal; it only burrowed sorrow deeper into the marrow. Each street, each voice, each smell of sugarcane reminded me of what I had lost, until even breathing felt like betrayal.

I had no kin to steady me, no friend to lean on. Being the only son, I had never been taught the art of standing alone. My parents had built walls around me to protect me from life's harsh winds. Now those walls had collapsed, and I stood naked before the storm—untrained, unprepared, unbearably human.

One morning, after yet another night of staring into the dark, I made my choice. The holy man had placed two paths before me—renunciation, or the world. My heart, wounded as it was, chose the world. *Let suffering come,* I thought. If it was to be my companion, then I would not flee from it. If my father's life had been claimed by the road, then the road would claim me as well. I would not resist the same destiny; I would embrace it.

With nowhere else to turn, I sought out my uncle in a distant town. He understood my brokenness and placed me as a helper on a lorry. The work was merciless: long hours, harsh weather, the endless stretch of roads disappearing into horizons that seemed to mock me. Yet, in that crucible, something hardened within me. Sweat became my prayer, fatigue my meditation.

Within months, I was no longer a shadow trailing my father's memory. I became a driver in my own right. And on the day I first held the wheel alone, with the road unrolling endlessly before me, something within me shifted. The world was no longer a place where I was merely surviving—it became a journey, vast and unknowable.

The lorry driver who trained me often spoke in ways that pierced deeper than mere instruction. One evening, as we shared tea in a dusty roadside stall, he said quietly, "The most important moment in a man's life is when adversity stands before him. That is where most hearts stumble. They waver, they doubt, and in their hesitation, they plant the seeds of greater sorrow. But adversity is not a curse—it is a question God places before us, asking: *Do you have the strength to choose?*"

I listened, the steam of the tea fogging my tired eyes, and he went on.

"My father always said that the power to choose right depends on the strength of one's intellect. A weak mind is a cracked mirror—it distorts everything it reflects. Fear creeps in, illusions multiply, and decisions lead only to regret. But a strong intellect is like a sword: it cuts through the fog of confusion and reveals the path hidden beneath."

He paused, as if weighing whether to reveal a deeper truth, then leaned closer.

"Do you know how intellect is cultivated? Not through grand gestures, but through small, faithful acts. Rising at dawn, not because the world demands it, but because the soul honours it. Praying, not as ritual, but as discipline of silence. Patience, not as a mask, but as the soil where clarity grows. Every little act we repeat chisels the mind into shape. And in time, the mind shapes destiny itself."

He looked into the distance, where the road shimmered in the heat like a river of fire. His voice dropped lower.

"My father warned me of one thing: never to accept a task just to prove myself, never to take on more than my spirit could hold. To do so, he said, is like drinking slow poison—it doesn't kill in a day, but it corrodes the soul until nothing is left. We are not here to impress the world; we are here to discover the truth of our own nature. If a fish is forced to climb a tree, it will die believing it was foolish, when in truth it was meant to swim in the vastness of the sea. Find your element, live within it, and you will flourish."

The words settled into me like seeds falling into the dark soil of grief. The road had taken much from me, but perhaps it was also giving something back. It was no longer merely tar and dust—it was becoming my teacher.

He paused, then leaned forward as if lowering a veil between ordinary talk and secret truth. "When I first stepped into the sugarcane factory," he said, his voice almost a whisper, "my father gave me one last piece of counsel. *Do your duty without compromise,* he told me. *Remember, nothing in this universe belongs to us. Everything is God's. Whatever you truly need will be provided. But the moment you begin to grasp, the moment you claim things as 'mine,' suffering begins."*

He exhaled deeply, his eyes lost in the fog outside, as though he were seeing not mist but eternity itself. Then he recited slowly, like a prayer remembered from another life:

This universe is pervaded by the Divine. Enjoy what is given with a spirit of renunciation. Do not covet what belongs to another.

Silence followed, heavy and all-pervasive. At last, he turned toward Ivaan. "Do you know what this means?"

His gaze held no demand, only depth. "It means nothing here is ours—not the soil beneath our feet, not the wealth we guard, not even the people we love. Everything is passing through us, like wind through open hands. And yet we clutch. We clutch as if life could be frozen, as if the world could be held still."

He tapped gently on the wooden counter, each knock echoing like a heartbeat. "Imagine a river. A traveller stoops to drink from it, but he does not claim the river as his own. He drinks what is given, then moves on. That is how life should be. But instead of drinking and moving forward, we dam the waters, clutch at their flow, and then suffer when the flood comes."

His voice softened until it was almost inaudible. "True joy is not in owning, but in releasing. Accept what comes to you. Love those who walk beside you. Fulfil your duties. But do not cling, do not command, do not demand. To love is not to chain; to work is not to expect reward. The instant you let go of ownership, life grows light. The more you grab, the heavier the world presses upon your shoulders."

He leaned back, his faint smile touched with sorrow. "My father knew this well. I did not. I wanted to keep everything—my home, my family, the illusion of certainty. But life stripped it all away. And in that nakedness, I learned: grief is not born of loss, but of resistance to loss. Nothing was ever mine, and so nothing was ever truly taken. That realization does not erase suffering—but it transforms it. What once felt like chains becomes wind. What once felt like theft becomes release."

His eyes returned to Ivaan, steady and luminous, as if they held the reflection of a road stretching into eternity. "The road itself teaches this lesson. Every journey has a beginning and an end. Every cargo you carry is not yours to keep—it is entrusted to you for a while, until it is delivered at its destination. Nothing belongs to you. Nothing stays. The sooner you learn this, the lighter your heart becomes, and the freer your steps will be."

The driver leaned back, his voice calm yet unwavering. "Do you know, I never feel disgusted—not even today?"

Ivaan tilted his head, listening.

"In storms, when the winds howl and the rains flood the roads, I ride my lorry without hesitation. Not for pride, not for profit, but because someone is waiting at the other end. I remember once, in the middle of a monsoon night, a medical consignment had to reach a small village hospital. The roads were drowned, many drivers refused to take the risk. But I knew patients lay there, helpless, their lives tied to the medicines I carried. So, I drove through water that reached my wheels, steady, prayerful, careful. When I finally delivered the supplies, I saw the relief in the doctor's eyes—it was as if I had delivered life itself. That day I understood: hardship loses its weight when it serves something greater than yourself."

He paused, letting the memory linger before continuing. "And I have given lifts to many along the way. Strangers, wanderers, the forgotten of the roads. One night I saw an old man shivering at a deserted bus stop. He had missed his bus and had no place to go. I stopped without a thought and let him in. As we drove, he spoke of his youth, of his dreams and losses, of time slipping through his fingers like sand. By the time I dropped him off, I felt as though he had given me more than I had given him. Before he left, he blessed me and said, *'Kindness never goes in vain.'* To this day, I carry those words with me."

His smile deepened, soft and steady. "And do you know? I have never truly met deceit on the road. People tell me the world is full of cheaters, but I have seen honesty more than lies. Just last week, a young man left his wallet in my truck. I drove back miles to return it. He was astonished—he even tried to press some money into my hands. I politely refused. His gratitude was enough. Encounters like these assure me—goodness has not left the world; you just have to choose to see it."

He turned toward Ivaan, his eyes gleaming with something more than light—it was conviction. "You see, my boy, life is about focus. What you choose to see becomes your world. I choose to see goodness, and so far, the world has not disappointed me."

The timbre of his voice shifted then, deepening like a drumbeat in the earth. The air itself seemed to grow still. "Now, listen carefully."

Ivaan felt the change at once. He straightened, folded his legs beneath him, and waited with wide eyes, as though sitting before a sage on the banks of a river.

The driver inhaled slowly, and when he spoke, it was not just a man speaking, but something larger moving through him: "I walk the path of *Karma Yoga*—the yoga of selfless action. Each deed of mine, however small, is not mine—it is an offering to the Divine. I do not act for wages or applause; I act because action is worship. Every morning, before I take the wheel, I bow my head and pray—not for wealth, not for comfort, but for strength. Strength to do my duty with honesty, sincerity and dedication.

My lorry is not merely a machine to earn a livelihood—it is my altar. My journey, my sacrifice. Each mile I drive is a prayer, each delivery a yajna (sacrifice).

Through these wheels and roads, I become an instrument of His Will. When the mind learns to act without clinging to the fruit, every hardship becomes light. Every burden becomes sacred."

"With this spirit, I drive my lorry through storms and scorching heat, ensuring that goods reach those who await them. Whether it is sacks of grain for hungry families or medicines for hospitals, I do not see my labour as mere livelihood—it is my worship, my yajna, my offering to the Divine. I perform my duty without clinging to the fruits, for the reward is not mine to demand.

Whatever I earn, I know, is not truly mine. It is born of the harmony of countless forces—the sweat of farmers, the toil of labourers, the skill of mechanics, the prayers of loved ones, the grace of the unseen Divine. I have come to understand that my earnings are not mine alone. They are a collective blessing. If I hoard them, I break the cycle. If I share them, I become part of the eternal rhythm. The Scriptures say: those who eat without sacrifice are thieves. But those who dedicate their share back to society, to nature, to the Divine, keep the wheels of creation turning.

This wheel has turned since the dawn of time—the sun offering light, the rivers quenching thirst, the trees bearing fruit without demand, every being giving itself so that life may continue. If I refuse to give, I become a burden. But if I offer my share with humility, I merge into the divine current, and become a true Karma Yogi.

I do not work for money, nor for recognition. I work as an offering. My only reward is the peace of mind that comes from service without attachment. And in that peace, I touch the highest goal of life."

"You see, my boy," the driver said, his gaze steady, "the mistake most people make is that they measure every action against the coin of reward. If they help someone, they expect gratitude. If they work hard, they expect praise. If they make a sacrifice, they expect blessings to fall upon them in return. But this is not the way of Karma Yoga. The true Karma Yogi asks for nothing, because he knows that every act is not his—it is an offering, surrendered at the feet of the Divine.

He lifted his eyes to the vast night sky, where stars shimmered like ancient witnesses. "Look at the sun—it burns, it gives light endlessly, never once asking, 'What do I receive in return?' Look at the rivers—they flow tirelessly, never demanding thanks from those who drink their waters. If human beings learned even a little from nature—to act without selfish motives—we would be free. Free from disappointment, free from worry, free from sorrow.

Now, listen carefully, for I will share with you the wisdom of Swami Vivekananda: 'Good, good; bad, bad; none escapes the law.'

Simple words, but within them lies the essence of existence. This is the law of karma—the eternal law of cause and effect. No action in this universe vanishes into nothingness. Each deed, like a seed, must sprout, must bear fruit. Whether we see it or not, every action sets forces into motion, and those forces circle back to us. Good actions bring harmony and joy; bad actions bring suffering and bondage.

But karma is not merely like Newton's law—push and pull, action and reaction. No, karma has deeper dimensions. Let me show you its three faces.

The first is the **Immediate Consequence (*Drashta-Phala*)**—the visible result of action. Feed a hungry man, and he feels relief. Smile at someone, and they return the smile. Speak harshly, and you awaken anger. These are the first ripples, the surface waves of karma, the fruits you can taste at once.

Yet, karma does not end there. Its second face is subtler—the **Mental Imprint (Samskara)**—the mark every action leaves upon the mind. Each deed, pure or impure, carves a tendency within, shaping who you are becoming.

When you feed the hungry man, ask: Why did I do it? If for show, then pride—not compassion—remains. Pride becomes your samskara. Next time, you will again seek eyes to witness, ears to praise. Ego hardens into habit.

But if you fed him with a silent heart, without expecting anything in return, then the samskara is of love, humility and purity. That seed will grow quietly within, making kindness more natural with every act.

For karma is not only about what you do to the world, but what the act does to you. Every deed is a stroke upon the canvas of your inner world. Just as rivers carve valleys, repeated actions shape the riverbed of personality. The selfish deepen grooves of greed; the generous carve channels of compassion.

And these grooves do not vanish with death. They endure, carrying fragrance or poison into future births. The scriptures call them vasanas—unfulfilled desires and tendencies that cling to the soul like shadows. This is why one child shows effortless kindness, while another hoards or wounds. It is not chance; it is the echo of past karma.

Now comes the third and most mysterious face of karma—the **Cosmic Reaction (Adrushta-Phala)**—the unseen forces that return to us from the vast ledger of existence. This is karma's deepest mystery: the universe remembers even when we forget. The energies we release into creation circle back to us, though not always in ways we can predict.

Think again of the hungry man you fed. If you offered him food with a pure heart, without even the faintest thought of self, that act becomes like a silent prayer released into the cosmos. The prayer does not dissolve—it travels, unseen, until the time is ripe. Perhaps years later, when you are broken and helpless, a stranger will step forth and give you exactly what you need, though you never asked. Perhaps in another life, you will be born in a place where hunger is a stranger to you.

And if the act was selfish—done for praise or recognition—its ripples will return as well. You may gain admiration for a while, but later find yourself exposed, ridiculed, or shamed, for truth cannot remain hidden forever.

We, in our ignorance, call these things 'luck'—good luck, bad luck. But there is no such thing as luck. There is only karma ripening in its own season. The universe is flawless in its memory, and its justice never falters.

That is why people ask: 'Why do bad things happen to good people?' or, 'Why do the dishonest prosper while the honest suffer?' The answer lies in the timing of karma. Not all seeds sprout at once. Some germinate quickly, others lie dormant in the soil for years, even lifetimes. A man may be rich today because of good deeds from long ago. But if he squanders that wealth with arrogance and cruelty, he is planting bitter seeds that will certainly bear fruit in time.

The wheel turns, my boy. Always. The only choice we have is what we place upon it."

A righteous man may suffer today, not because of what he does in this moment, but because of seeds sown in some forgotten yesterday. Yet if he persists in walking the path of selfless duty, if he keeps his steps steady in the direction of truth, then the future—whether in this life or another—cannot deny him peace. Justice may be slow, but it is inevitable.

By now the eastern sky had begun to blush—a deep red spreading across the horizon—yet its warmth struggled to pierce through the heavy fog that wrapped Delhi in silence. The lorry driver rose without ceremony. He did not linger for thanks or recognition, nor did he wait for Ivaan's reply. The distant hum of an approaching crowd told him the stall would soon awaken to the bustle of voices. Without another word, he walked briskly to his truck, turned the engine on and vanished into the mist, as if swallowed by the very fog that had birthed him.

His words did not carry fragrance of scripture, nor the grandeur of saints. They were plain, even rustic. But in their simplicity throbbed a profound rhythm—the rhythm of karma lived, not preached; of duty embraced without bargaining; of surrender without name or form.

And Ivaan, sitting there with the rising steam of tea in his hands, felt the weight of it settle into his heart. What he had just witnessed was not a sermon but Karma Yoga itself—alive in grease-stained hands and weary eyes. The universe, he realized, does not always send teachers wrapped in saffron robes or seated upon thrones of wisdom. Sometimes it speaks through a truck driver, a roadside encounter, a chance word on a fog-laden morning.

For the one who seeks, every encounter is scripture, every stranger a messenger. The universe is never silent; it is only the ears of the distracted that fail to hear.

Ivaan understood, dimly yet unmistakably, that this lesson had come to him not by chance. The cosmic play had woven this meeting into his journey long before he had stepped into that stall. Every soul who walks towards realization is guided—gently, secretly, but without fail.

Because before consciousness can reveal its radiance, the mind must first be swept clean. And the broom the sages speak of is not silence alone—it is selfless action. To serve without desire, to give without asking, to love without clinging.

Only such action has the power to hush the restless mind. And only in that silence does the Self unveil itself.

8
The Veil of Maya

The universe never grants its bravest souls the mercy of an easy path. Comfort is not their inheritance, nor silence their dwelling. Instead, the cosmos awakens their minds into storms, shattering the fragile walls of certainty until every question blazes like fire. Then, as if conspiring with destiny itself, it sends luminous souls along the way—teachers in disguise—who scatter fragments of wisdom, hints of truth that come like sparks in the dark.

But the universe is never satisfied with half-measures. Having fed the seeker with glimpses of the eternal, it summons the world to reveal its grand illusions—the *maya*. It spreads before him the majesty of desire, the intoxication of power, the indulgent dance of attachment. It allows him to taste beauty until he confuses it with truth. And just when his heart clings to the dream most tightly—life snatches it all away, leaving him shattered, stripped, and naked before the abyss.

For the bravest are tested by the sharpest blades. To forge a sword strong enough to cut through illusion, the fire must be merciless. And so it was with Ivaan.

In the fields where he grew up, among the humble shepherds and the endless skies, there were countless souls content with their bread, their cattle, their songs of the evening. But Ivaan was not like them. His heart was restless, his gaze questioning. Where others saw only grass and sky, he saw riddles of existence. Why are we here? What is this fleeting play called life? What lies beyond the veil of death?

The child of shepherds had dared to question the kingdom of heaven itself. And for that audacity, destiny had chosen him—not to walk an easy road, but to be hurled into the heart of *Maya*, where illusions are sweetest and chains invisible.

Three months had passed since Ivaan first set foot in *Sharma Ji*'s modest tea stall, and in that short span, life itself seemed to have shifted its rhythm.

What was once a humble roadside corner, offering only steaming cups of tea and a few dry biscuits, had blossomed into a gathering place alive with voices, stories, and the fragrance of food. The clinking of cups, the hiss of frying oil, and the laughter of strangers painted a portrait of unexpected prosperity. Travelers paused, businessmen lingered, and even the respected of the city now found reason to sit upon those wooden benches.

To *Sharma Ji*, this was nothing less than a miracle. For years, he had struggled, his little stall surviving but never shining. Yet now, as he watched the crowd spill into the mornings and evenings, his eyes would often rest upon Ivaan with gratitude. "Luck changed the day this boy arrived," he whispered to himself, though in his heart he knew it was more than luck. There was a strange gravity around the boy—as if life itself tilted in his presence.

But for Ivaan, the real transformation was not in the stall's fortune, but in the silent revolutions within his own soul. Two encounters in these months had struck him like lightning bolts across the night sky.

The first was with Dr. Iyer, a philosopher whose words were not merely spoken but carried the weight of centuries of thought, shaking Ivaan's understanding of what it means to live. The second was far humbler—an exchange with a weary lorry driver who, without robe or scripture, revealed the essence of karma and selfless duty through the raw poetry of lived experience.

Neither encounter was accidental. Ivaan felt it in his bones—these were not random passings, but carefully placed stones upon his path.

He began to see that the universe, in its mysterious wisdom, speaks not only through sages and saints, but also through truck drivers, tea sellers, and chance meetings in the fog.

And yet, beneath the clatter of teacups and the glow of the morning sun, Ivaan sensed something more. These months were not an arrival, but a preparation. The wheel of destiny had begun to turn, and he could almost hear it grinding beneath the surface of his days.

Just as the lorry vanished into the mist that morning, Ivaan felt himself on the verge of vanishing too—not into nothingness, but into a journey far greater than he could yet imagine. A journey that would strip away illusions, test the strength of his heart, and throw him into the very arms of *Maya*—the beautiful, the intoxicating, the destructive.

The tea stall was prospering. Life appeared to be kind. But deep within, Ivaan knew the truth: the real storm had not yet begun.

Although Ivaan sensed that the true storm of his life had not yet begun, he could not imagine the force with which it would strike one day. For now, life unfolded with a deceptive smoothness, as though the universe itself was conspiring to make his path gentle.

Among the shepherds of his village, he had risen as a quiet leader, admired not only for his strength but for the depth of his questions—questions that went far beyond fields and cattle, into the very fabric of existence. His father walked beside him as both guide and philosopher, shaping him with counsel that blended wisdom and love.

And then came Saira. She was beauty made of flesh, and in a single glance she captured Ivaan's heart. Her presence opened a door he had never known before—a longing so sweet it felt divine, yet so consuming it carried the seeds of bondage. Love made the ground beneath his feet both steadier and more perilous.

With this new-found confidence, Ivaan's steps carried him into the city, where the humble tea stall of *Sharma Ji* transformed under his care into a vibrant meeting place. Life seemed to reward his devotion. Along the way, he crossed paths with enlightened souls—teachers in disguise—who poured fragments of eternal wisdom into his eager mind.

It appeared, outwardly, as though destiny was smiling. He had knowledge, respect, prosperity, and even the stirrings of love. Yet beneath the surface, the grand design of *Maya* was silently at work. For what is *Maya*, if not the art of binding the soul with silken threads of sweetness—making the prison feel like paradise, until the day the walls collapse?

The boy, still so young, had already touched heights that many never glimpse in a lifetime. And with each passing day, a shadow grew within him—quiet, almost invisible at first—the strengthening of the ego. This was not a fault of his alone; for in youth, when the world bends easily to one's will, the ego rises like a hidden tide.

Where ego awakens, desire soon follows. And where desire takes root, attachments bloom. Ivaan, who once walked with a seeker's clarity, now found his mind painting pictures of a sweeter future. Dreams began to ripple through him—dreams that whispered of permanence in a world built on transience.

He imagined returning to his homeland, standing before his father with pride, and confessing the secret flame he carried for Saira. He imagined asking for her hand, binding her presence to his destiny. And Delhi, which once felt like a mere station in his journey, now appeared as a place to settle, a stage for prosperity and comfort. The tea stall's earnings—greater than any shepherd could have hoped for—fed these dreams. Soon they glowed with the illusion of certainty.

But *Maya*'s genius lies in this: she does not come with chains, she comes with flowers. She does not frighten the soul, she soothes it with visions of love, success, and belonging. And Ivaan, like every soul before him, began to mistake the comfort of the veil for the light of truth.

When a man tastes even a drop of success, the ego swells as naturally as the river rises with rain. Most never notice it, for they are busy delighting in its flood. But the seeker is different. His victories are not merely rewards; they are tests in disguise. For the ego that grows unnoticed is the first veil of *Maya*—the quiet hand that turns the gaze of the soul outward, away from its own source.

Why, then, would the universe allow this to touch Ivaan, who sought truth with such hunger? The sages say: the Divine does not test the indifferent; it tests the earnest. The world tempts most men to bind them, but it tempts seekers to free them. Just as fire must first consume the wood before light can emerge, so too must the seeker be entangled in illusion, only to awaken through its unravelling.

Thus, it was not cruelty that placed desire in Ivaan's heart, but design. The universe was not closing the door of realization; it was placing him on the threshold. For only when a man mistakes the mirage for water, and suffers the thirst that follows, does he truly seek the wellspring.

With desires and dreams stirring quietly within, Ivaan felt an urge to journey to the land of Gods—Rishikesh. To the unknowing eye, it seemed a pilgrimage born of faith, a young man drawn to the holy banks of the *Ganga*. But beneath the surface, the currents of *Maya* had already begun their silent work. For *Maya* does not always pull a seeker into darkness through obvious temptations; often, she cloaks herself in the sacred, leading one towards light only to test whether he sees the flame or mistakes the smoke for fire.

And so, with a mind full of questions and a heart weaving dreams of love, prosperity, and freedom, Ivaan set his gaze toward Rishikesh. He thought he was walking toward the Gods. In truth, he was walking into the next layer of the grand illusion—the dance of *Maya* herself.

One late evening, as the tea stall quietened, Ivaan turned to *Sharma Ji*, who was busy counting the day's earnings. His heart beat heavily, as if urging him towards words that could no longer be held back.

"*Sharma Ji*," he began, his voice steady but tinged with hesitation, "may I speak with you?"

Sharma Ji looked up, his weathered face glowing with its usual warmth. "Yes, my son? What is it?"

Ivaan drew a breath, then spoke with quiet resolve. "I wish to visit Rishikesh for a few days. Would you allow me leave for this?"

For a moment, silence lingered between them. Then *Sharma Ji*'s eyes softened, and a knowing smile curved his lips. "Of course, you must go," he said, without a trace of reluctance. "How could I ever stop you from answering a call that is not of this world? From the day you arrived, I knew you were not meant to remain behind this counter. You brought prosperity here, yes—but I sense the stall was never your destination. Your journey is written on a far vaster canvas."

Ivaan blinked in astonishment. He had expected questions, perhaps resistance—but instead found only blessing.

Sharma Ji placed a fatherly hand upon his shoulder. "Go, Ivaan. Walk the path that summons you. And may the Gods themselves reveal what you are seeking."

The next morning, beneath a pale rising sun, Ivaan set forth. His frugal belongings rested lightly in his bag, but his heart carried a weight of dreams, questions, and unspoken desires. As the bus wound its way through the misty Himalayan foothills, a hush seemed to descend upon him. Villages blurred into forests, forests melted into rivers, and each turn of the road felt less like distance travelled and more like layers of himself being peeled away.

Rishikesh—the land of sages and seekers, where the *Ganga* herself whispers eternal truths—awaited him. Yet, Ivaan did not know that he was not merely going to Rishikesh; he was being drawn into the power of

Maya, into a trial that would test every dream, every attachment, and every illusion he had begun to weave.

Ivaan did not know where he would stay in Rishikesh, but he had heard that many ashrams opened their doors freely to wandering seekers. Carrying no burden of worry, he walked towards the banks of the *Ganga*, drawn by the sound of bells and chants that filled the air like a hymn of the universe itself.

When he reached the ghats, he found hundreds gathered—monks draped in saffron, pilgrims with folded hands, and travellers whose eyes brimmed with longing. They had assembled for the evening *arati* (ritual term) to the sacred river. Not knowing the rituals, Ivaan simply joined the throng, letting the collective devotion carry him. The flames of the oil lamps flickered like stars descending into the river, the chants rose and fell like waves, and the air was thick with incense and surrender.

When the worship ended, the crowd slowly dispersed—some to their ashrams, some to their homes, others further along their journeys. Ivaan, however, remained seated on the cold stone steps. He wished to linger, to let the majesty of the *Ganga* etch itself into his being. The river, praised in a thousand hymns, now flowed before his eyes—vast, unending, ungraspable.

It was then that an old monk appeared. His beard was long, his eyes deep as still water, his robe the colour of fire. He paused beside Ivaan, studying him for a moment, and then spoke in a voice at once gentle and piercing.

"What are you doing here, child? Your age is not for sitting on the banks. The time for you to renounce has not yet come. The world is calling you—go back, engage, serve. When your hour arrives, the river itself will summon you."

The words struck Ivaan like a riddle wrapped in command. "Is this the way monks speak?" he wondered. I have harmed no one, I merely sat to witness the river—why then did this old man bid me to leave, as though my presence disturbed the flow of destiny?

Finding his voice, Ivaan replied with quiet hesitation. "I am from Kashmir. For now, I serve at a tea stall in Delhi. Soon I shall return to my homeland. But before I do, I felt called to visit this sacred place. That is why I am here."

The monk regarded him in silence, then asked, "And where do you stay in Rishikesh?"

"I have not decided yet. But I will find a place to stay," Ivaan answered.

A faint smile touched the old man's lips. "Then walk with me. You may stay where we reside. No roof shall cost you here. Only your food you must provide."

Both walked in silence. The monk's steps were steady, measured, as though he had walked these paths for centuries. Ivaan, beside him, felt the night grow heavier with each turn of the road.

Just before they reached the ashram gate, the monk suddenly stopped. He turned, his eyes glimmering in the dim light of the oil lamp, and spoke in a voice that cracked like thunder across a still sky:

"Very soon, child, you shall be caught in the vast net of *Maya*. The power that binds gods and men alike will come upon you. Your desires will be tested, your dreams broken, your heart struck with loss. I see your life on the verge of being shattered. Return to Kashmir while you still can—before the storm claims you."

The words fell upon Ivaan with the weight of fate itself. He stood frozen, his chest tightening, unable to breathe freely. *Maya*? Storm? Shattered dreams? He could not digest such ominous prophecy. A part of him resisted—perhaps this is how old monks speak, freed of the world, their tongues free to utter anything that crosses the mind.

And yet… the words clung to him like shadows. That night, when food was offered, he found no appetite. When he lay down to rest, sleep would not come. The monk's voice echoed within him—deep, unsettling, unshakable—like the low rumble of thunder that warns of a storm yet to break.

The next morning, the ashram was alive with movements. Monks moved with quiet discipline, preparing for a session to be delivered by a revered master *Swami Atmananda Ji*. Though Ivaan had come to Rishikesh with the simple thought of visiting sacred places, something ignited within him, compelling him to join the gathering.

The hall fell into a hush as the master entered. Tall and dignified, his very presence was a sermon in itself. His posture radiated both strength and serenity, his handsome face glowing with an inner light, as though he carried the dawn within him. Draped in flowing saffron robes, he seemed less a man and more a living flame of truth.

He began with the customary prayer, his voice calm yet commanding, each syllable vibrating through the silence like ripples upon still water. Then, after a pause deep enough to draw every soul into its gravity, he spoke.

"Why do people suffer?" His voice reverberated like a bell across the hall. "Why does arrogance take root in the human heart? Why does ego, like an unquenchable fire, consume clarity and peace? Why is man never satisfied—always hungry for more wealth, more power, more recognition? Why does he cling to fleeting pleasures, chasing happiness in objects, only to find it dissolving like mist? Why do desires multiply endlessly, each one giving birth to another?"

Ivaan leaned forward, his heart pounding. The very questions mirrored his own unspoken restlessness.

The master's eyes swept over the assembly, luminous and steady. "Even in this age of great scientific progress, these fundamental riddles remain unsolved. Science explains how the world functions, but it does not reveal why man is enslaved to longing, why suffering clings to him like his own shadow. The answer, my children, lies in *Maya*— the great illusion. It is *Maya* that paints the unreal as real, the temporary as eternal, and the false as true. It is *Maya* that binds even the wise, weaving a net of appearances that entangles the soul in an endless embrace."

Ivaan felt a chill run through him. His mind echoed with the monk's warning the night before. Twice now, in less than a day, the word had come to him—*Maya*. He could no longer dismiss it as coincidence. It was as though destiny itself was whispering: *This is the storm you must face.*

It was not a lecture in the usual sense. The gathering felt alive, breathing with questions unspoken and answers flowing like the river outside. The revered Master did not speak to instruct, but to awaken. His words rose not as declarations, but as responses to the silent yearning of those seated before him. At times, a monk would raise a query. At other times a seeker would nod. And sometimes the hall would fall into a silence deeper than speech.

The Master began:

"*Maya* is not just attachment or desire. It is the very fabric of experience itself. It is what makes the fleeting seem eternal, the unreal appear real, and the limited appear limitless. Through its veil, you mistake shadows for substance, and temporary joys for eternal happiness."

He paused, letting the silence deepen. A young monk spoke gently, "But Master, is *Maya* only this world of possessions and attachments?"

The Master's eyes softened, and his voice echoed like a quiet thunder. "To say that is to reduce the ocean to a cup. *Maya* is far more subtle. It is not merely bondage, not merely suffering, not merely wealth or name. It is the grand illusion itself— the stage on which life's drama unfolds. It cannot be grasped directly, only seen through its effects: the endless craving, the cycle of joy and despair, the arrogance of ego, the fear of loss."

The seekers sat unmoving, as though bound by the weight of unseen truths. Ivaan felt the words pierce straight into the unease he had carried from the night before.

The Master's tone grew quieter, almost intimate. "In *Advaita Vedanta*, *Maya* is one of the pillars, but no scripture dares define it fully. For the moment it is defined, it slips away. One does not know *Maya* by words — one sees it in the restless heart, in the dream of permanence, in the tears that flow when impermanence strikes."

He looked around, then smiled faintly. "Perhaps a story will help."

The assembly was all ears.

"Once, the sage *Narada* begged Lord *Krishna*: 'Show me the truth of *Maya*.' *Krishna* smiled, but gave no answer. Days later, while they walked through a desert, *Krishna* said, '*Narada*, I am thirsty. Bring me some water.'

Narada went to a village. A young woman opened the door. The moment their eyes met, *Narada* forgot—forgot *Krishna*, forgot his quest, forgot even himself. That moment became a day, the day became a life. He fell in love, married, had children. Twelve years passed. He tilled lands, reared cattle, sang lullabies at night. He lived a life full, complete, rich with joys and sorrows…"

The Master's words trailed off, hanging in the silence like a riddle left unsolved.

The Master's voice slowed, becoming almost a whisper, as though he were guiding everyone into a dream.

"Then, one night, a flood came. The river rose like an angry bull, swallowing the village in its fury. Houses dissolved, animals were carried away, screams filled the night. *Narada*, clutching his wife in one hand and two children in the other, tried to fight the waters. Another child clung to his shoulders as he waded through the current.

Step by step, he struggled — but the torrent was merciless. The child on his shoulders slipped into the black waters. *Narada* cried out, but as he reached to save him, another child was torn away. His wife's hand, too, slipped from his grasp, disappearing into the flood.

One by one, everything he loved was devoured by the river. Alone, broken, he was cast ashore. His sobs shook his body; his world was shattered; his heart turned to ashes."

The hall fell utterly silent, as though the grief of *Narada* had descended on every soul present.

The Master continued softly: "At that very moment, a familiar voice called from behind him: '*Narada*, where is the water? You went to fetch a pitcher of water, and I have been waiting for you. It has been half an hour.'

Narada turned, stunned. *Krishna* stood before him, just as he had left him. The village, the wife, the children, the lands, the flood — all of it had vanished, like mist in the morning sun. Twelve years of life had passed in the space of thirty minutes.

"This," the Master said, his gaze sweeping across the assembly, "is *Maya*. The dream you call reality, the reality you mistake as eternal. It is the play of the infinite, where lifetimes unfold in moments and moments stretch into lifetimes. It binds, it blinds, and it breaks — until one awakens."

"Now," the Master continued, his voice steady and reflective, "let me explain it in greater detail." He spoke without pause, drawing deeply from Swami Vivekananda's teachings.

"Saints die; sinners die. Kings pass away, and so do beggars. No one escapes death. Yet, a fierce clinging to life grips us all. Why is that so? We do not know, and yet we hold onto this transient existence as though it were permanent. This—this mysterious contradiction—is *Maya*."

He paused briefly, letting the silence expand like a mirror for the minds listening.

At this, the old monk who had brought Ivaan leaned forward. His voice was weathered, almost like dry leaves brushing the ground: "Master, if everyone sees death, if no man can escape it, why does the heart still cling to life? Is *Maya* stronger than truth itself?"

The Master smiled faintly. "No. Truth is never defeated. But the brilliance of *Maya* is in her disguise. She does not deny truth—she simply veils it. Like clouds that cover the sun, she makes what is eternal seem hidden, and what is fleeting appear as eternal."

The gathering fell deeper into stillness.

"Death moves through this world day and night," the Master went on. "It whispers behind every breath, every heartbeat. And still, we walk as if we are untouched by it, as if eternity is our inheritance in the physical form. We see others depart every day, their lives fading like embers in the wind, but we convince ourselves that our flame will burn forever."

A younger monk, unable to restrain himself, asked softly: "But Master, if everything perishes, why were we made to desire? Why were we given hearts that long for permanence?"

"Because," the Master replied, his gaze steady, "that longing is not for the perishable. The soul seeks the eternal, but in its forgetfulness, it clutches at shadows. And shadows cannot quench thirst. This is *Maya*'s play."

He took a slow breath, allowing the truth to sink deeper.

"And in this illusion, we plunge headlong into the chase—for wealth, for position, for name, for security. In the pursuit of power, we trade peace. In the desire for more, we forget what we already have. We compromise joy for gain, truth for comfort, and love for pride. This is *Maya*—not merely a veil, but a theatre of shadows, a perfectly orchestrated dream in which the unreal appears more enticing than the real."

The hall was still. It was not silence of absence, but of presence. Something sacred was being felt.

A strange fear gripped Ivaan's heart. Against his own will, words escaped him: "But Master… if everything is only a shadow, then what remains real? What is left for us to hold on to?"

The Master turned toward him gently, eyes filled with compassion. "That which does not die, Ivaan. That which no flood, no flame, no shadow can erase. The Self—pure, infinite, untouched. But until we see it, *Maya* will keep staging her theatre, and we will keep mistaking the play for the Truth."

Then, with a knowing smile, *Swami Atmananda Ji* recalled a timeless dialogue from the *Mahabharata*: "King *Yudhishthira* was once asked, 'What is the most wonderful thing on this earth?' He replied, 'Everyday, people die around us, and yet men think they will never die.'"

The words fell into the hall like drops of truth into a still lake.

"From the very moment we are born," he continued, "we are thrust into the field of struggle. We arrive into the world with a cry—a declaration of life, and at the same time, a subtle reminder of the battle ahead. And then one day, without warning, death arrives. It takes us—whether as victors or vanquished, we cannot say. It comes not with a warning, but with quiet certainty. And this, too, is *Maya*."

He paused, his tone softening but carrying deeper weight.

"Look at the hope in a child's eyes," he said. "The world glows like a golden dream, the future an untouched canvas. He believes his will alone can paint it. But as he grows, he meets the unyielding laws of nature. Obstacles that do not bend to desire. Dreams that drift away like mirages. He strives, he struggles, and yet—death arrives again, not as an enemy but as a reminder: the chase was never the point. The striving itself was the illusion. And this, too, is *Maya*."

He looked around the hall, not as a teacher above his students, but as a fellow traveller who had seen through the mirage and yet walked with love for those who hadn't.

"Then," he continued, "consider a man of science. He rises not by chance but by an unquenchable thirst—a striving for knowledge, for mastery over nature. No sacrifice is too great, no night too long. He unravels mystery after mystery from the sacred vaults of creation..."

And yet, a question lingers—haunting and persistent. *For what purpose?*

Why do we glorify man? Why must the world revere the discoverer, the inventor, the one who claims to have pierced the veil of the unknown? What is the source of this admiration?

Nature, vast and silent, performs miracles far grander—without effort, without applause. She brings forth life from dust, hurls lightning across the heavens, and flings stars into the void with a majesty we can never match. And we, who barely scratch the surface of her workings, who only copy and rearrange fragments of her design, stand upon stages and call ourselves creators.

We tame a current and call it electricity—while nature has been weaving thunderbolts since the beginning of time. We name laws of motion and gravity—while planets have spun, danced, and collided under these very forces long before we could count the hours of a single day.

Still, we race ahead and call it progress. We wear the badge of achievement, never questioning the illusion we serve.

And this, too, is *Maya*.

The illusion that blinds not only the ignorant but also the brilliant. The deception that paints imitation as originality, and discovery as creation. It whispers to the mind, *"You are the doer,"* when in truth, nature remains the silent architect—indifferent to praise or blame.

At this point, one of the monks raised a hand. His voice was gentle, yet uneasy: "But Master, if everything is nature's doing, if we are but imitators—does not our striving have meaning at all? Is it all just vanity?"

Swami Atmananda ji smiled, his eyes kind but piercing. "The striving itself is not vanity," he replied softly. "It is the identification with the *striver* that is vanity. To act without clinging, to discover without pride, to create without ego—that is not *Maya*, but liberation from it."

He let the silence settle, and then continued:

"The senses, like skilled thieves, pull the soul outward—away from its centre. They lure us into a labyrinth of desires, pleasures, and fleeting joys. They promise happiness at every turn, only to leave us empty in the end.

For ages, sages have warned us: true happiness does not reside in the outer world. The pursuit of pleasure is a mirage. Yet, humanity learns slowly. We must taste the bitter before we see the truth.

So we chase. We indulge. We fall. And when grief strikes, we awaken—briefly. But like moths to the flame, we return to the dance of delusion, believing perhaps this time the fire will not burn.

Each fall is followed by a rise—stronger, more desperate, more determined. We call it resilience, not realizing it is the persistence of illusion. And so the wheel turns—again and again—until the soul, weary of the chase, collapses not in defeat but in quiet realization.

And this, too, is *Maya*."

Our intellect—so celebrated, so trusted—is not exempt from the grasp of *Maya*. Just like the senses, it too entraps. It spins a subtler web—not of pleasures and desires, but of thoughts and questions. The human mind is a restless tide, forever surging forward, yearning to know, to solve, to possess the hidden workings of the universe. We assume, almost blindly, that every question must have an answer, that the reservoir of knowledge is bottomless, waiting only for our effort to draw it forth.

But in this pursuit, we meet a quiet truth—one that stands like a sentinel at the edge of our reach. We take a few steps along the path of inquiry, only to find ourselves halted by something vast and immovable. We run into the endless stretch of time—an expanse with no beginning and no end. We stare into the fathomless sky and find no edge, only more sky. We realize, perhaps with unease, that all of existence unfolds within an unrelenting law: cause and effect, action and consequence, birth and death.

And try as we might, we cannot break the chain. Still, we continue. Still, we seek. Still, we hope. This, too, is *Maya.*

We walk as though free—making choices, speaking words, chasing dreams. We believe ourselves to be independent agents, shaping our destinies. But with every breath, every decision, every heartbeat, the illusion begins to flicker. We are bound—by instinct, by habit, by conditioning. Nature dictates our body, the mind dictates our thoughts, and our desires dictate our direction.

We are not moving freely; we are being moved. And this, too, is *Maya.*

Even where love shines the brightest, illusion often hides in plain sight. A mother's love—unquestioned, celebrated, revered—seems the purest flame. She looks at her child and sees a miracle. She lives through him, feels his joy, absorbs his pain, and would sacrifice everything for his smile. But what if that same child, as time unfolds, moves away? What if he forgets her kindness, speaks words that cut deep, returns love with indifference?

Still, she cannot stop loving him. The more he wounds her, the deeper her heart clings. The world sees this and applauds—it calls it divine, unconditional. But few pause to ask: is this love, or is it bondage dressed in virtue?

Her love is no longer a choice—it is compulsion. She suffers, but cannot detach. She aches, but cannot escape. She decorates her pain with words of sacrifice and names it sacred. Yet within, she remains bound—not by her son, but by the illusion that she *must* love, no matter the cost.

And here, too, *Maya* reveals herself.

The hall grew still. The Master's voice, until now a scalpel, grew soft and tender: "Maya is not merely illusion. It is the sacred power through which the supreme consciousness, *Brahman*, brings forth the dance of creation. By the veiling and projecting force of *Maya*, the infinite appears as finite, the nameless takes on names, and the formless becomes a world of forms. It is through *Maya* that this vast universe unfolds, woven with stars and sorrow, birth and becoming. Yet at the heart of it all, nothing has truly changed.

Vedanta proclaims with unwavering certainty: our real nature is divine—pure, perfect, eternally free. We do not become *Brahman*—we are *Brahman*. The *Atman*, our innermost Self, is not separate from the absolute reality. It is that same reality, clothed in the illusion of individuality."

Ivaan, his voice trembling, finally asked: "Then why, if we are already divine, are we so tragically unaware of it? Why do we stumble through life like sleepwalkers, trapped in fears, desires, and suffering?"

The *Swami*'s eyes softened. "The answer lies in *Maya* itself—in the power of ignorance. *Maya* is the veil that hides the truth of our being. It operates through two subtle forces.

The first is ***Avaraṇa Shakti***—the power that obscures. It is like clouds concealing the blazing sun, hiding *Brahman* from our sight.

The second is ***Vikshepa Shakti***—the power that projects. It builds an illusion, conjuring a world of duality and delusion. It makes us see a snake where there is only a rope. It makes us believe, with all our heart, that we are the body, the mind, the ego."

His words fell like drops of thunder. "Together, these two powers entangle us in a dreamscape. We mistake the unreal for the real, the fleeting for the eternal. We become trapped in the web of name and form, and in doing so, forget who we truly are."

He paused, then his tone deepened. "*Brahman* alone is real—the silent, unmoving ground of all that is. The *Upanishads* declare: *'All this is indeed Brahman.'* Like images on a screen, the changing world borrows its seeming reality from the changeless substratum behind it. Without that silent witness, the show cannot go on."

The *Swami*'s gaze swept the hall. "But our perception is distorted—warped by time, space, and causality. Conditioned by the body, we dread sickness and decay. Conditioned by the mind, we chase pleasure and flee from pain. Conditioned by the ego, we build fortresses of pride, greed, and fear. And all the while, the real Self—the *Atman*—remains untouched."

He lifted his hand, as if parting a curtain. "*Maya* is like a dense fog. It doesn't destroy the sun; it only hides it. In the same way, the Self is ever-present, ever-radiant. We do not need to become anything new—we only need to remember. And that remembrance begins when the fog begins to lift."

His voice grew gentle, like wind stirring the trees. "Spiritual practices—deep meditation, unselfish service, purity of heart, and unwavering inquiry—are the winds that clear the sky. With each breath of truth, the veil grows thinner. With every act of compassion, the illusion weakens. When we turn inward and ask, 'What is real? What am I?'—we begin to pierce the fog of *Maya*."

He leaned forward, his words now a whisper. "Adi Shankaracharya gave a timeless example. A man walking at dusk sees a snake on the road. Fear rises, his heart races. But with light, he looks again—and sees only a coiled rope. The fear dissolves. The snake was never real; it was only an illusion."

The *Swami* closed his eyes. "So it is with us. Walking the dark path of delusion, we see a fragmented world—we suffer, we fear, we cling to the temporary. But when we truly look—deeply, steadily—we discover that the world, the self, and all of existence are nothing but *Brahman* in disguise.

The snake dissolves; the rope alone remains. The illusion dissolves; *Brahman* alone remains. And in that awakening, all separation falls away.

Only Oneness remains."

As the discourse came to an end, a hush lingered in the air—a silence so profound it seemed more eloquent than words. It was not emptiness, but presence—like the pause between two heartbeats, holding the weight of eternity.

Ivaan sat motionless. He had come seeking answers, but what he received was something deeper: a glimpse into the veil that had shaped his every experience. The stories, the metaphors, the voice of the monk—all had pierced the restless surface of thought and entered the hidden chambers of his being.

A strange calm washed over him. The struggle he had always carried—the relentless pursuit of meaning in the outer world—suddenly seemed misplaced. For the first time, his inquiry turned inward: *Who is this "I" that sees, desires, suffers, and dreams? Who is the witness of all this play?*

The image of the snake and the rope returned to him vividly. He almost felt his body recoil again, his heart racing. How often had he, too, lived in the grip of shadows mistaken for threats? How many times had he clung to ambitions and affections, mistaking them for permanence, only to watch them dissolve like mist in sunlight? Could it be that his entire life had been a dance of illusions spun by *Maya*?

Yet, this realization did not crush him. A gentle disillusionment arose—not despair, but clarity. It felt like dawn breaking: the recognition that freedom was not to be found in accumulation—of possessions, knowledge, or power—but in uncovering what had never been absent: the still, unchanging Self beneath the shifting noise of mind.

He understood now: *Maya* was no mere concept. It was the invisible puppeteer that had bound him to fear, ego and desire. But if *Maya* had the power to bind, then awareness must hold the power to set free.

As he stepped out into the cold evening, the world looked unchanged—the mountains still brooding, the river still flowing—but something within him had shifted irrevocably. He was no longer merely a seeker chasing distant truths. He had begun to awaken.

Not fully—not yet. But the veil had quivered, and through the faintest tear, a strand of light had seeped in.

9

The Lens of Illusion

Ivaan had come to Rishikesh dreaming of sanctity—the holy land where sages had walked, where gods themselves had left their imprints on stone and river. He expected serenity, revelation, perhaps even bliss. Instead, the city revealed to him a mirror he did not wish to see. What began as a discourse on *Maya* was no longer just an echo of the monk's words; it had become the air he breathed.

The temples felt hollow, the hymns sounded like distant echoes, the forests loomed with an uneasy stillness. Even the *Ganga*, whose waters he believed would cleanse him, appeared restless, as though carrying secrets beyond his grasp. Wherever he turned, the same shadow followed—the whisper of *Maya*.

It was not philosophy anymore; it was pursuit. The veil he thought he had glimpsed was now tightening around him. His mind, once eager for answers, grew restless with doubt. His heart, once seeking joy, grew heavy with unease. And somewhere deep within, he sensed a truth more terrifying than ignorance itself: that the power of *Maya* does not merely hide the Real—it takes hold of the unreal and makes it feel inescapably true.

The descent had begun.

The next morning, Ivaan boarded the bus to Delhi. The wheels rolled forward, but his heart refused to move. It was a storm within him—a thousand questions swirling within him, no answer steady enough to hold them. The monk's words had not left him; they clung like echoes in a cave, rising again and again in the silence of his mind. *Maya... the veil, the great deceiver...*

The road ahead stretched endlessly, winding through villages and fields. But Ivaan felt as if he were being pulled backwards—towards something unfinished, something waiting. Life, he realized, had never obeyed the commands of his restless will. The universe moved according to its own law, indifferent to his longings.

And then it struck him—*Maya* was not always thunder and lightning. It often arrived in soft disguises: in comfort, in routine, in the certainty that tomorrow will look like today. Its grip was strongest when least suspected. He shivered. *What test awaits me now? Not outside—but inside?*

By the time the bus reached Delhi, dusk had begun to spill over the city. Ivaan's feet carried him instinctively to the tea stall—the place that had become his refuge, his hearth. He remembered *Sharma Ji*'s booming laughter, the way he used to tap Ivaan on the shoulder and call him "the miracle boy." How many evenings had they sat together in the fragrance of chai, weaving stories that made the world feel less heavy?

But today, the stall stood silent. The shutters were down, locked from the outside.

Ivaan stopped. His throat tightened. "Four o'clock…? This can't be," he muttered. The stall was never closed at this hour. Never.

He looked around for familiar faces, and finally, one of the shopkeepers met his eyes. The man's gaze was heavy, his lips trembling as though holding back a flood.

"Ivaan…" he whispered, his voice breaking, "*Sharma Ji* is no more. Yesterday evening… a heart attack…"

The words fell like iron into Ivaan's chest. For a moment, he could not move. His legs weakened, his breath faltered. The world blurred at the edges—shops, people, even the air around him seemed to dissolve.

No. Not him. Not Sharma Ji.

His mind rebelled. He saw, in flashes, *Sharma Ji*'s laughter, the way his wrinkled hands stirred the boiling tea, the kindness in his eyes when he listened as though Ivaan's troubles were the only thing that mattered in the world. All those moments rose like a tide—and then shattered against the cruel finality of death.

Ivaan staggered back, clutching the edge of a wall. Inside him, two voices tore at each other. One screamed: *How can this be? Life is unjust. Why would God snatch away the one soul who gave me warmth, who called me his own?* The other, quieter but merciless, whispered: *This is Maya. Did you not hear the monk? All that you cling to—friendship, love, certainty—will crumble. What you saw as lasting was but a dream.*

Tears burned in his eyes. He wanted to cry out, to curse the heavens, to beg for one more cup of tea with *Sharma Ji*. Yet another force held him—an unbearable silence, the kind that strips away even grief. It was as if *Maya* herself stood before him, unveiling her true face: not just illusion, but the ruthless hand that snatches away what you love most.

The bustle of Delhi carried on around him. Cars honked, people bargained, children laughed in the distance. But Ivaan stood still, hollowed out, as if time itself had paused to mock him.

And in that emptiness, he realized: this was the true beginning of the test. Not in temples, not in forests, not in the monk's words—but here, in the raw tearing of the heart, where *Maya* whispered: *Cling, suffer, despair.*

Without wasting another moment, Ivaan rushed toward *Sharma Ji*'s house. His breath quickened with every step, as if his heart already knew the truth that his mind still resisted.

As he reached, the air itself seemed heavy, saturated with grief. Wails rose and fell like waves, heart-wrenching cries that clung to the walls and spilled into the street. The house, once so warm with *Sharma Ji*'s laughter, now stood draped in silence broken only by sobs—a silence that spoke of absence more loudly than presence ever could.

At the doorway, Ivaan froze. His body would not move forward. The sight before him was unbearable—*Sharma Ji*'s wife, broken and inconsolable, clutched by relatives who struggled in vain to calm her. The air was thick with sorrow, every breath heavy with the weight of loss.

After a few moments, summoning courage that felt alien in his trembling limbs, Ivaan stepped inside. The world seemed to blur around him, voices distant, only grief magnified.

The moment *Sharma Ji*'s wife saw him, something shifted. With a cry that came from the very depths of her soul, she tore herself from the arms that held her and rushed toward him. She collapsed into his chest, clinging to him as though he were the last remnant of her husband's life.

Her words came like daggers, each syllable cutting deeper than the last: *"Had you not gone to Rishikesh, this wouldn't have happened! You were his lucky charm... Why did you leave him? Why, my son, why?"*

Ivaan's breath paused. Guilt surged through him, hot and suffocating. His chest ached not only with his own grief but with the unbearable burden of being seen as the cause of another's suffering. The accusation, born of pain, pierced his heart in ways no philosophy could prepare him for.

The images rushed back—the tea stall alive with laughter, *Sharma Ji*'s booming voice, the endless cups of chai that had carried their conversations into the night. That little corner of the city had been more than a shop. It was a temple of companionship, of simplicity, of warmth. Now it stood empty, never to be the same again.

Ivaan could not walk away. His soul would not allow it. The weight of grief in that household pressed against him like an immovable stone, but beneath it was something stronger—a quiet vow of love and gratitude. He decided to stay. Not out of duty, not out of obligation, but out of reverence for the man who had given him shelter when he was adrift.

Through the long night of mourning, he sat in silence with the family. He listened to the whispered memories, the broken fragments of conversations now frozen in time. His presence became a wordless comfort, a reminder that *Sharma Ji*'s kindness had not vanished with his body, but continued to live in the lives he had touched.

When the final rites were performed and the smoke of the pyre drifted into the sky, Ivaan felt a strange hollowness within him—as if part of his own being had burned with it. Yet there was also clarity. Death had revealed what *Maya* always concealed: the fragility of all that we hold dear.

At last, with quiet resolve, he told the family he must return. "The grazing lands will be ready by now," he said softly, "and the sheep will be waiting." Life, indifferent and unyielding, had already begun to move forward. Grief could not halt its current.

But Ivaan knew something within him had changed forever. The illusion of permanence had been shattered. He carried with him not only the memory of *Sharma Ji* but also the sharp awareness of *Maya*'s power—the ruthless reminder that what we love most can be taken away in an instant.

The next morning, Ivaan boarded the train back to his village.

The train moved along the same tracks, yet nothing felt the same. Outside the window, fields stretched endlessly, the rivers glistened, and the horizon rose and fell as it always had. But within him, a storm brewed. The journey that had once been familiar now felt foreign, hollow.

No familiar voice sat beside him to break the silence. No warm words of wisdom filled the air. Only the rhythmic clatter of wheels on rails accompanied him—each turn of the wheels echoing the weight of his thoughts.

For the first time, Ivaan felt the raw ache of true loss—a wound too deep for time, too sharp for wisdom. He had faced setbacks before, but this was different. This was not life refusing to bend to his will. This was life snatching away something irreplaceable.

His mind wandered back to the tea stall—the endless cups of chai, the warmth of *Sharma Ji*'s laughter, the wisdom that once seemed like stories but now burned like truth. He thought of Khushwant Singh's words before dawn, of the old monk's haunting warnings. At last, they began to settle inside him—not as philosophy, but as reality.

"This is life," he thought. *"Unpredictable. Fragile. Always slipping through our fingers. The moment we hold it too tightly, Maya reminds us—nothing belongs to us."*

The train screeched to a halt, shaking him from his reverie. He stepped down onto the platform, his body heavy yet restless. Ahead lay the road to his village, to his father, to the embrace of home—or so he hoped.

But as the village came into sight, his heart sank. From a distance, it looked... altered. Shadows hung over it like a storm that refused to leave.

When he finally stepped inside, devastation spread out before him. Houses broken, walls crumbling, the air thick with dust and despair. Women wept openly, their cries merging with the wails of children. Men sat amidst the ruins, staring blankly at what once was their home.

Before he could make sense of it, a few villagers rushed to him. Their eyes were swollen from grief, their hands trembling as they clutched at him. They cried into his shoulders as if he were the only solid ground left.

Confused and breathless, Ivaan tried to ask what had happened. Their sobs gave him no answers—only more dread. He could only imagine a storm, merciless and wild, sweeping through and tearing apart all that was familiar.

Heart pounding, he broke free and ran—past broken walls, past families mourning their losses, past the weight of devastation pressing down like an invisible mountain. His chest burned, but his legs carried him faster, toward the only place that mattered—his home.

And then, like a blade slicing through his frantic search, a whisper found him.

Soft, but sharp enough to pierce his very soul.

"Your father is no more."

The world stopped. Time itself seemed to fall silent.

Ivaan stood frozen, his breath caught between disbelief and despair. The earth beneath him felt unsteady, as though *Maya* had pulled the very ground from under his feet. In a single moment, all that tethered him to life—mentor, guide, father—had dissolved into the same merciless silence.

The world around him blurred. The ground beneath his feet felt as though it had vanished, leaving him suspended in a void of silence. A silence so heavy it pressed against his chest, suffocating him.

No one was there in the house to grieve. The rooms stood hollow, stripped of their warmth, their emptiness louder than any cry. His father's absence was not just felt—it was like a wound carved into his very being, raw and unbearable.

The villagers had already performed the last rites. The fire had burned, the ashes had scattered, and with them, every chance of a final word, a final glance, had vanished. There had been no waiting for him, no pause for his return. Life had moved on without him. He was too late.

Ivaan collapsed to the ground, his limbs refusing to move. His heart pounded in his chest, but his spirit felt deadened. Regret tore through him like a storm. *Why did I leave? Why did I abandon him for my selfish wanderings? Had I not been so blind, so foolish, I would have been by his side when he breathed his last.*

Tears flooded his face, his cries shattering the suffocating silence. He lifted his trembling hands towards the sky, pleading, demanding, raging: *"What wrong have I done to deserve this? What crime could life punish me so mercilessly for?"*

Villagers came to him, moved by his grief. They lifted him gently, carried him to one of the repaired houses, and tried to console him. But their words were like rain falling on stone. Nothing reached him. Nothing could touch a heart that had shattered beyond repair.

"Life never strikes so cruelly unless one is cursed," Ivaan whispered to himself, blaming his own existence.

His father had been everything to him—protector, guide, companion, anchor. With him gone, the very ground of his being had collapsed. *"How do I live now? There is no reason left to live,"* he murmured, his voice hollow, drained of all will.

Days passed. The village stirred with the rhythm of life again. Men rebuilt broken walls, women gathered grain, children ran barefoot through the dust. The storm had scarred them, but it had not stopped them. Life, relentless and indifferent, pressed forward.

But Ivaan remained unmoved. His ruined house stood like a monument to despair, and he sat before it in silence, staring at stones and dust as though they mirrored the ruins of his own heart.

Neighbours cared for him, brought him food, spoke words of encouragement, urged him to rise, to rebuild. But to Ivaan, their voices were distant echoes, dissolving into the void within him.

Yet, beneath the weight of grief, something faint began to stir—like a fragile flame struggling to survive the winds. He realized no tears, no sorrow, no curse could reverse death. His father was beyond reach, beyond time, beyond him.

Life, whether cruel or kind, did not release him. His time had not come. He could not escape living.

And in that bitter recognition, a seed was planted: the beginning of surrender.

Not to despair, nor to death, but to the truth he could no longer ignore—that life is not his to command, that loss is not his to resist, that existence itself must be borne until its purpose is fulfilled.

There was no other option left for him but to rise—rise from the ashes of his grief and step forward. His father was gone, but life, ruthless in its demand, insisted he moved on. He had to rebuild, not just his home, but himself. The bread must still be earned, for life waits for no one.

After a few days, when Ivaan had somewhat regained his composure, the well-wishers of the village began urging him to marry and start a family. Some even brought proposals, hoping to see him weave himself back into the fabric of life. But Ivaan refused. His heart was too heavy, his wounds still too raw. The thought of marriage felt distant, unreal—like asking a broken wing to take flight.

Yet, as days stretched into weeks and the requests kept coming, a quiet name surfaced in his heart. Saira.

Saira, the daughter of a peasant—the girl he had seen once while returning the sheep. He had never forgotten her presence, like a sudden breeze on a suffocating day. There was a grace about her, a kindness in her eyes that had lingered in him like an aftertaste of something sweet.

But then came the doubt. *What am I, but a shepherd? How dare I dream of someone like her?*

Still, hope, fragile and persistent, whispered against his despair. Perhaps fate, having taken so much from him, might grant him this one joy.

The season of grazing returned. Shepherds from across the villages gathered with their flocks, ready to begin. Ivaan joined them—not just to tend his sheep, but with a silent prayer burning in his heart.

At the peasant's house, where sheep were collected, he stood watching the familiar bustle of men, voices, and bleating animals. But his eyes searched for only one thing. His heart beat faster with each passing moment. Would he see her today?

Saira.

Her name rose within him like an old melody, haunting and beautiful. Unable to resist, he wandered restlessly, waiting for even a glimpse. But she was nowhere.

At last, unable to bear the silence of not knowing, he turned to a villager and asked about her.

The answer came casually, without weight—yet it fell upon Ivaan like thunder. "Saira got married."

For a moment, the world stopped. His breath snapped, the ground beneath him hollowed, and everything around seemed unreal. His heart, which had quietly nurtured a fragile dream, cracked under the truth.

She was gone.

The dream had dissolved, like mist touched by sunlight.

The girl he had once hoped to see again—the one who had unknowingly become a symbol of something beautiful in his life—was now only a memory.

A bitter smile flickered on his lips. How mercilessly the universe played with him! Just when he thought he was beginning to rise from his grief, life had found yet another way to remind him of his insignificance.

Dreams, he realized, were never meant for men like him.

Ivaan sank to the ground, his gaze lifting toward the vast, indifferent sky. His father was gone. *Sharma Ji*—who had once called him a miracle—was no more. And Saira, the quiet hope of his heart, had slipped away into a life where he did not belong.

Every door had closed. Every road had dissolved into emptiness.

Only the flock of sheep remained. Only the valley stretched before him—eternal, silent, unmoved. The sheep would hear his voice but would never answer. The valley would echo his cries but would never console.

For a long moment, Ivaan sat hollow, the wind moving through him as if he were already a ghost. Then, slowly, he rose.

This was *Maya*—the grand illusion. That which gives, only to take. That which binds, only to break. That which makes the heart believe, only to remind it of its own fragility. He had heard of its power. Now he had felt its claws.

And yet… the world did not pause. The river flowed. The wind blew. The sheep grazed.

And so, emptied of everything yet still breathing, Ivaan walked ahead.

10
The End of Duality

The valley stretched before him—silent, familiar, and rich with memory. Once it had cradled his childhood joys; now it held the weight of his losses. The sheep moved slowly across the grass, heads bent, oblivious to the storms in their shepherd's heart.

Ivaan walked among them, haunted by a single question: *Why do we suffer?*

He had lost his father. He had lost the fragile hope of Saira. He had even lost the belief that life held meaning. The valley was unchanged, the sheep grazed as they always do. But within him, a fire burned, a hunger for an answer deeper than fate or chance.

Had humanity not wrestled with this very question for ages? Saints, poets, and sages had sought the root of suffering, yet it clung tight to every heart. And as Ivaan's gaze followed the restless flock, the old monk's words returned: *The root of suffering is duality.*

The mind divides: gain and loss, praise and blame, joy and grief. Like sheep scattered in opposite directions, it runs endlessly, never at rest. A child is branded "good" or "bad." A man is weighed by "wealth" or "poverty," "success" or "failure." Even love becomes a bargain—who gives, who withholds. The mind thus remains split, yearning, afraid.

This was *Maya*—the endless play of opposites that traps the soul in its web. And Ivaan could feel its grip on his life more than ever.

Yet, in the silence of the valley, another possibility bloomed. If the mountains stood unmoved by shadow or sunlight, could not the Self also remain untouched by joy or sorrow? Was there not a way of being beyond the restless swing of the mind?

Perhaps, beyond the play of opposites, there was wholeness—a truth the world could neither give nor take away. And as he walked among his sheep, Ivaan felt the first stirring of that deeper quest: the search for the end of duality.

Ivaan sat on a rock, his eyes following the sheep as they grazed lazily across the meadow. Their world was simple—no judgments, no comparisons, no restless swing between hope and despair. Watching them, a question ignited within him: Was human suffering nothing more than this pendulum of opposites—pleasure and pain, joy and sorrow, success and failure?

There must be a way, he thought, where the pendulum stops. Where the mind rests, not in choices and outcomes, but in presence. A path that does not deny the world, yet refuses to be entangled by it. A vision that sees beauty in both sunrise and storm, that knows success and failure as two waves rising and falling in the same ocean.

This was not passivity but, clarity—a realisation that beneath all changing appearances lay something untouched. Call it Consciousness, the Self, *Brahman*. That which witnesses every experience and yet is never stained by it.

He closed his eyes, trying to feel the valley wind brush his skin. Were pleasure and pain truly opposites, or merely passing ripples in the same field of awareness? The mind judged, the body reacted—but was he the sum of those reactions, or the silent watcher behind them?

His thoughts drifted to something he had once read in a book on science. Even neuroscience seemed to echo this truth. The brain is wired for duality: the amygdala flares at danger, the prefrontal cortex weighs right and wrong, safe and unsafe. Dopamine lit up with reward, while the insula and cingulate burned with the pain of rejection.

The brain is a mirror of *Maya*—mapping life in opposites, weaving survival out of division. No wonder humanity lives in conflict. The very organ through which reality is seen is wired to split it.

Ivaan opened his eyes. The sheep moved in unison now, clustering as if they sensed something he did not. The valley lay unchanged, yet a subtle shift had taken place within him. For the first time, he felt—not as thought, but as truth—that there was a way beyond the endless swing of opposites.

Not escape, but awakening.

Even science seemed to whisper of it. The brain's circuitry of fear and desire, pain and pleasure, was not fixed. With awareness, with training, it could change.

He remembered reading once: when the mind rests in non-judgmental awareness, the brain itself begins to rewire. Circuits of reactivity fall silent. Networks of presence awaken. The sages called it meditation. Scientists called it neuroplasticity. Different tongues, same truth.

We are not doomed to be slaves of the pendulum. The brain itself can learn to rest in balance—to witness without grasping, to see without being shaken.

And if that was so, then the ancient promise was real: what we seek has always been within us. Even science, at last, nodded in agreement.

There were rare ones who had walked this path—men and women unmoved by praise or blame, joy or sorrow. They did not flee the world and yet were not bound by it. They lived in a stillness untouched, no matter how fortune's winds blew.

This was not indifference—it was clarity. Clarity that saw dualities for what they were: a dance of appearances, a play of forms. And while the dance continued, awareness rested vast, unmoved.

This was the third path—the path of pure awareness. There was nothing to be gained, but a state of mind where gain and loss are irrelevant. It's always here. Subtle, unchanging, free. The moment it was recognized, even for a flicker, suffering dissolved.

For Ivaan, the recognition was dawning. His long night of trials had not been a curse, but a hidden boon. The universe had led him into fire not to destroy him, but to purify him—to test his surrender, his trust in that unseen thread that holds all things together.

In the vastness of existence, his suffering was no tragedy—only a ripple in the great ocean, a passing scene in the endless play of the cosmos. Loss and longing, despair and hope—none of these were his alone. They were currents moving through all beings. The universe did not mourn or rejoice; it simply allowed these currents to move unhindered.

And then, like dawn breaking quietly over a horizon, a deeper truth revealed itself: time was not real. Not an absolute law, but a projection of mind, stitched from memory and imagination. The universe was not moving from past to future. It simply was—still, silent, eternal.

Life was not a road to walk, but a presence to awaken to. The suffering had never belonged to him. Pain had never truly touched what he is. It was all part of the divine play—and he had only been the witness.

The first light spilled across the mountains, gilding the peaks, softening the valley. A deep stillness rose within him. The weight he had carried for so long dissolved into the sky. For the first time, he was not resisting. He was not searching.

He was simply watching.

Nothing remained that he could call his own. No home awaited, no arms stretched out to hold him in an embrace, no dream pulled him towards an imagined future. The past had faded like a forgotten tale, and the future had no shape. All that remained was this moment: breath in his chest, sheep grazing nearby, breeze in the valley, the endless sky above.

And in that emptiness, he found something unexpected—lightness. Freedom. With nothing left to cling to, nothing left to lose, he felt untouched. Grief and longing had melted away like mist in the morning sun. What remained was bare, honest, whole.

The world could no longer chase him, for it had nothing left to take. A man without desire cannot be tamed by suffering. Ivaan had become such a man—not through denial, but through the quiet erosion of everything he once thought was essential.

He was no longer an actor in the drama of becoming. He had become a witness—still, aware, free. The play unfolded, yet he no longer mistook it for reality. In that pure watching, he tasted something sacred, something timeless.

True freedom, he realised, was not escape or resistance, but surrender. Not the absence of trials, but the absence of struggle. The universe does not test souls to break them, but to refine them. Those who cease resisting are carried to the quiet shores of peace.

Then clarity struck: no force, not even *Maya*, can bind a man who desires nothing. Such a man cannot be owned, cannot be controlled. He is free because he is whole within himself.

The flock grazed in silence, their presence a wordless scripture. They did not speak, yet carried a wisdom older than thought. In their stillness, they reminded him that life, like the seasons, never ceases to turn—that every loss holds the seed of something new. Their companionship asked for nothing, yet gave everything: trust, presence, an assurance that he was not alone.

They stood around him patiently, sensing his stillness. Their hunger tugged gently at his heart, calling him back into the rhythm of life. In that pull, Ivaan awakened from the trance of sorrow. The past had dissolved, the pain had vanished and life was calling him forward.

He gathered the flock and led them towards the open grasslands, where the first blades of green rose from the thawing earth. Winter had passed. The valley was breathing again.

Perhaps this—this simple act of care, of presence—was enough. Perhaps in living without demand, without clinging, he had already touched what so many seek for lifetimes.

Evening fell softly, wrapping the valley in a hush. The flock followed Ivaan without command, their quiet order mirroring the strength of their shepherd. Days folded into nights, nights into days—time no longer pressed upon him. Grief, once heavy, now slipped away—not because the memories were gone, but because they no longer held weight. Like snow surrendering to spring, sorrow had completed its work.

And in the stillness that remained, Ivaan turned his eyes inward. He saw the mind as a restless river, flowing only with thoughts, each of them born from desire. It fluttered from branch to branch, never content. Yet the witness within him did not stir. He began to see: he was not the river, but the sky through which it flowed.

The mind directs the senses outward—to see, hear, taste, touch, and smell. The senses return with impressions, and thought takes form. Desire arises, spilling into speech and action, circling endlessly. For most, this is life's cycle - thought, speech, action—repeating itself without pause.

But what happens when the senses bring nothing back? When the eyes find no delight, the ears no melody? The mind resists silence. It rummages through memory, revives old pleasures, replays old wounds, spins fantasies—anything to keep itself alive.

The mind does not care whether the body suffers or rejoices. Its only mission is to continue—seeking, consuming, leaping from one desire to the next.

Yet now, Ivaan was watching from a distance. He saw its schemes, its hunger. And slowly, something within him began to rise—not in defiance, but in clarity. The mind was not his enemy. It was only untamed. In the light of awareness, even the restless river could be understood. And in understanding—transcended.

Days passed like pages of an unseen book, each lighter than the last. Ivaan no longer measured time by cold or bloom. Something had shifted—subtly, like a tide turning suddenly, like dawn breaking after a moonless night.

Once, he thought suffering was an enemy to be conquered. Now he saw: freedom lay not in resistance, but in seeing through it. Pain and pleasure were ripples on the surface of existence—arriving, lingering, passing. What remained was the witness: the still, untouched awareness beneath it all.

The Ivaan who once clung to dreams and wrestled with despair was only a memory now, a shadow of a self that had never truly existed. He no longer chased happiness or feared sorrow. He had begun to live in the still space beyond opposites, where light and dark, gain and loss dissolved into a single, indivisible truth.

He walked the same paths, heard the same winds in the trees, tended the same flock. But everything was different—not because the world had changed, but because he had. Life was no longer measured as good or bad. It simply was. And in that being, peace arose—so profound that even the mountains seemed to bow to it.

Ivaan had moved beyond the veil of duality, the play of opposites that once bound him. He saw now that the world was not divided. It was whole. There was no other, no enemy, no saviour. Only this moment, and the silent witness within it. That witness—unchanging, eternal—was who he truly was.

Life itself had become the answer. Thoughts still came, but no longer ruled him. Emotions arose, but no longer shook him. The secret was not hidden in distant scriptures, but in the simplicity of breath, of presence, of surrender.

When the sun dipped behind the hills and the stars blinked awake, Ivaan would sit beneath the vastness and smile—not in joy or sorrow, but in quiet knowledge. He was no longer the seeker. He had become the act of seeing itself.

And still, life continued—the sheep grazed, the wind moved, the river flowed. But Ivaan, once a man aching for meaning, now belonged to it all. Nothing to gain, nothing to lose. Only the gentle rhythm of being.

This, perhaps, is what it means to live beyond suffering: not to escape it, but to stand so deeply rooted in awareness that nothing can move you. To live beyond duality is to rest in the silence from which both pleasure and pain arise.

In that silence, Ivaan was home. In that silence, we all belong.

PART THREE

The Horizon of Truth: Beyond Space-Time

11
The Witness Emerges

Ivaan could have gone back. Delhi waited with its smoke and chatter, *Sharma Ji's* tea stall stood ready to welcome him into the rhythm of small transactions. Rishikesh offered ashrams, chants and the safety of surrender. Even marriage might have provided a veil thick enough to keep the memory of Saira at bay.

But he did not return. He chose the sheep and the meadows. He chose silence over noise, the narrow path over comfort. The decision was neither dramatic nor deliberate. It was like breathing—something deeper chose for him.

Nights in the valley sharpened that choice. The wind moved through the grass as though it were a vast instrument, each blade trembling with a hidden music. His flock pressed close against the dark, and he felt himself pressed close to something vaster still—something watching, something waiting.

Such moments visit every life, arriving quietly. Most pass them by. A few pause, uncertain. Fewer still listen. Ivaan listened.

There is always a figure who turns aside from the march, and we remember them—not because they sought rebellion, but because their steps fell in rhythm with something larger. Crowds dissolve into anonymity; the one who steps away leaves a mark. Even history moves this way: not by the weight of the many, but by the silence of the few.

The valley seemed to know. It leaned towards him, as if the earth itself bent around his solitude. Even the sky felt conspiratorial, whispering its question through the constellations: Is this all there is?

The question lingered, and in its whisper, something shifted. He began to sense that he was not the one who watched, but the one being watched—that behind his solitude there was another presence, silent, immense, unblinking.

The witness had begun to stir. Ivaan was among those rare few. Not by ambition, but by alignment. Not by force of will, but by the quiet depth of his being. He was not merely a wanderer or a shepherd among sheep—he carried a silence older than himself, as if he had walked here across lifetimes. The world, trembling in its own transition, seemed to have summoned him—not to declare truths, but to embody them.

Such beings do not draw attention. They do not need to speak often, or heal with gestures. They move like hidden rivers beneath the soil, unseen yet altering the landscape above. Solitude is not their exile; it is their natural ground.

Ivaan may not have known this fully. But the valley knew. The trees leaned closer when he passed. The sheep followed not only out of habit, but as if sensing an ancient keeper. Winds carried his silence like incense through the meadows. Even the stars above seemed to pause, blinking in acknowledgment.

After storms and losses, desire loosened its grip. *Maya* no longer tempted him with its endless disguises. The world's noise receded until it was only a faint murmur. In that stillness, something began to stir—not thought, not feeling, but a presence blooming like dawn behind the eyes. It was less a discovery than a remembering, a whisper older than memory itself.

Who am I? What is this universe?

The questions rose, not from ego's hunger, but from a deeper thirst. Unlike worldly cravings that bind, this longing set him free. It burned with no agenda but truth.

And as the veil of duality thinned, he began to watch the mind itself. He saw how it rushed like an overeager scribe, stamping names and stories onto what was nameless. A tree, a river, a face—before thought touched them, there was only raw presence. Then came the words, the judgments, the memories. With them, the real slipped away.

For the first time, he glimpsed the gap between the world and the mind's version of it. Reality was not the story he carried about things. It was the silent fact of their being, here and now. Everything else was mirage.

Even science echoes this mystery. They ask: *If a tree falls in a forest and no one hears it, does it make a sound?*

Ivaan had pondered it once, staring at the dark ridge of pines. The wind bent their branches. Yet, in the silence of his watching, he wondered: was sound there in the tree, or only in the ear that receives it? Without a listener, the falling remained only a shiver in the air, a ripple in existence unnoticed.

Life was the same. Without the one who perceives, what is this tree, this body, this moment? Ivaan did not read this truth in books or hear it in sermons. It came to him wordlessly, like dawn seeping into stone. He felt it in the stillness where thought paused: the seer and the seen were not two. There was only what is.

Reality did not arrive as definition but as presence—simple, indivisible, beyond the reach of the mind. The sheep grazing at his feet, the wind brushing his skin, the stars blinking above—none of these were objects before him. They were himself, seen from a thousand angles.

Yet the valley gave him no explanation. There was no teacher around to confirm his vision. Its silence was his only guide. The sheep grazed, asking nothing. The mountains held their vigil as they always had. The wind whispered across the grass, carrying secrets too old for words.

And the two ancient questions rose again and again within him: *Who am I? What is this universe?* They did not come as curiosities, but as sacred fires. They were not asked to be answered. They were asked to awaken.

Ivaan sat still, his spine rooted in the earth like an old tree that had seen countless seasons. He had not sought silence; silence had sought him. It settled around his shoulders like a cloak. Even the sheep, scattered in the meadows, grazed without sound, as if the hush had entered their wool.

The river moved on—neither hurrying nor arriving—flowing because flowing was its nature. The breeze wandered the valley without aim, brushing against grass and stone simply because it could. The mountains stood unmoved, and yet their stillness seemed alive, listening.

Then he turned his eyes inward. His eyes could behold the flock, the mountains, the sky—yet never themselves. And yet he knew them. He could tell when they were weary, when they stung with smoke, when they brightened with joy. Who, then, was it that knew?

Ivaan closed his eyes and let his awareness descend inward, like water seeking the hidden source beneath a riverbed. One by one, he observed each layer of his being, naming it, noting it, and letting it pass: Not the body—its aches, its warmth, its hunger, its fleeting movements—none of this was him. Not the mind—its endless thoughts, its cravings, its doubts, its recollections—they came, they went, like waves breaking on the shore, yet he remained untouched. Not the breath that rose and fell, not the heartbeat that drummed a quiet rhythm, not the eyes that glimpsed the sky or grass or flock. Not even the act of seeing, nor the awareness that saw, nor the awareness of that awareness. Step by step, layer by layer, he let each "I am this" dissolve into a wider emptiness. The mantra of negation whispered through his mind: *Neti, neti—not this, not this.* And with every passing thought, every fading sensation, every dissolving self-image, the ground beneath perception seemed to widen. He glimpsed a still, unshakable presence—neither body, nor mind, nor breath, nor thought—yet containing all of them. Vast as the valley, radiant as dawn, and silent as the stars, it was not something to attain. It was the very space in which all things arose. In that luminous void, Ivaan finally understood: he was not the instrument of life, but the witness behind it, the eternal "I am" in which the entire cosmos unfolded.

The teaching of the sages echoed in him, not as a borrowed thought, but as lived fact: the seen is many, the seer is one; the seen changes, the seer remains. And that seer—silent, steady—was himself.

The hush of the valley deepened. Ivaan closed his eyes. His breath slowed until he could hear the faint thrum of blood in his ears. His hands twitched once, then stilled. Even the weight of his body on the ground seemed distant, as if it belonged to someone else.

The senses faded into the background, yet something remained to notice their fading. His mind was watching. It knew when his eyes burned with unshed tears, when his fingers trembled, when his chest rose and fell. The body changed, the mind observed.

But then another shift occurred. The mind itself grew restless, chasing fragments of memory and desire. Images flickered before breaking apart—his mother's voice, the missing star, Saira's smile. And yet, even as these thoughts rose and vanished, something deeper stayed untouched.

He realized: *I know that I am thinking.* He knew when his mind was agitated, when it stilled, when it darted like a startled bird, when it returned like a calm tide. But who was it that knew?

The question rang through him, clear and unshakable. And in its echo, he felt it—the witness. Not a thought, not a memory, not an image, but the presence behind them all. Silent. Unchanging. Awake.

Thoughts flickered like stars at dawn. Emotions passed like clouds dissolving in the sky. But the witness did not move. It had never moved. It simply was.

Unlike the eyes or the mind, the witness did not shift. It watched without judgment, without effort. Nothing it saw could stain it. It was not many, nor even one among many. It simply was—the clear presence behind every breath, every thought, every flicker of sensation.

Ivaan felt it as though stepping into a space he had always carried. It was not an idea, not a vision, but a ground—calm, unchanging, free. In that presence, truth glowed with a quiet certainty: he was not the body, not the mind. He was the awareness in which body and mind rose and fell like waves upon a shore.

And then the old question rose again, the one he had heard in whispers since childhood—the riddle of the forest disciple: *By whose will does the mind turn towards its objects? By whose command does the breath stir? By whose power do men speak? Who guides the eye and the ear?*

These were not curiosities of philosophy, he now understood. They were cries of the soul to know its Source.

And in the silence that followed, the master's ancient words resounded within him—not as scripture, but as his own seeing: *It is the ear of the ear, the mind of the mind, the speech of speech, the life of life, the eye of the eye.*

The answer pointed nowhere outside. It drew him inward, peeling back the layers of seeing and hearing, past thought and memory, until only the witness remained—the one light by which all else was known.

The disciple had known: the mind could not be sovereign. If it were, no man would walk willingly into his own sorrow. And yet, how often had Ivaan seen it in himself? The mind, clear on consequence, still rushing towards the very fire it feared. Wanting and regretting in the same breath. Choosing against its own wisdom. Lamenting what it had itself willed.

Such contradiction revealed it plainly—the mind, too, was not the final knower. It was observed, just as the senses were.

And in that recognition, something deeper unfolded. What had the master said? *Not the seen, not the heard, but that by which all seeing and hearing are known.*

Ivaan felt it now—not as thought, but as presence. A witness untouched by action, yet allowing all action. Consciousness itself, not as a concept, but as the very ground of his being. The mystery was no longer to be solved. It was to be lived.

A memory came: as a boy he had once left water in a brass vessel by the fire. Hours later, it was warm to the touch, though the flame had never touched it. So too, he saw, the mind borrowed its light. Breath, senses, thought—each shimmered with a radiance that was not their own.

By themselves, they were mere instruments—mute as a flute without breath. But something moved through them, animating, singing. The Self. The hidden musician.

The words of the sages ignited within him like an echo from eternity, though he had never studied them. *The ear of the ear, the mind of the mind, the life of the life.* They spoke of a Presence behind every faculty, a witness beyond all witnessing. The senses, the mind, even breath itself—he saw them now as instruments, like rooms in a house built for an unseen master. The Self was that master. The unthought thinker. The silent ground of all experience.

And in the stillness, he felt the truth the scriptures had whispered for ages: *Brahman shines by His own light. By His light all this is illumined.* The stars glittered above the valley, but he knew their glow was borrowed. The real radiance was the one by which even starlight was seen. *Who could live and breathe if there were not the self-luminous Brahman?*

The realization did not merely bring clarity. It loosened chains. For what could be lost if he was not the body? What could be wounded if he was not the mind? Immortality was not in children, possessions, or power—it was here, in the still Self, free of desire. The ancient voices seemed to move through the wind: *Not by works, not by offspring, not by wealth, but by renunciation alone is immortality attained.*

Ivaan sat unmoving. Yet, centuries of knowing seemed to rise within him like dawn. He was not alone. Across ages, others had asked, others had dared. He saw in his mind's eye the hall of King Janaka, where the sage *Yajnavalkya* once stood. And opposite him, a woman—*Gargi*, daughter of *Vachaknu*—her voice cutting through convention, her questions aimed not at the man, but at the mystery itself.

As Ivaan sat in stillness, the valley around him seemed to dissolve. And in its place, another scene arose—not of his making, but as if memory older than memory had stirred. He saw a court, luminous with firelight and silence, where sages and kings gathered.

A woman stood there—*Gargi*. Her eyes were steady, her voice unyielding. She did not ask about ritual or reward, about gods or heavens. She asked about that which holds even gods and heavens within its embrace:

"What is the thread on which all worlds are strung—above and below, past, present, and future?"

The hall stilled. *Yajnavalkya*, unmoved as a mountain and radiant as the midday sun, lifted his eyes. Step by step, his words rose—from water to air, from sky to sun, from gods to the womb of the cosmos—each answer dissolving into something higher, finer, until words themselves began to tremble at the edge of silence.

And then, pointing beyond all phenomena, he spoke:

"That, O Gargi, which is above and below, within and beyond, past and future—is pervaded by the unmanifest ether. And what pervades that ether is the Imperishable—neither seen nor heard nor grasped, but by which all seeing, hearing, and knowing take place. It is untouched, yet all is touched by It. It is unknown, yet It alone is the Knower."

The court fell into awe. *Gargi* bowed—not in defeat, but in reverence. The debate was not ended, it was transcended. Truth had spoken, not to conquer, but to liberate.

The vision faded, but its echo remained in Ivaan's heart. He recalled other words, ringing across time: Lord *Krishna*'s voice in the Gita, whispering of the Self—unborn, eternal, ancient, unchanging. *As one lays aside worn-out garments and puts on new, so does the Self take up forms and discard them.* The body perishes, but That remains—untouched, infinite.

Weapons could not cut it, fire could not burn it, water could not wet it, nor could wind dry it.

Ivaan saw it now—the Self, imperishable, beyond all elements, beyond time and space. It did not move, yet it was swifter than thought. It remained ever the witness—without beginning, without end.

He knew then: the one who realizes this does not slay, nor is he slain. Even in the midst of action, such a one abides in stillness. What perishes was never truly born; what is born is never truly absent.

The Self was subtler than the subtlest, greater than the greatest, dwelling in the silent cave of the heart. To know it was to transcend sorrow, to silence fear, to stand free amidst the rise and fall of worlds.

As his awareness deepened, the questions rose—not from doubt, but from wonder. If this inner freedom had been touched by sages across time, could it point toward a truth that binds all things—a theory of everything, hidden not in stars or equations, but in consciousness itself?

And in this vast cosmos brimming with countless beings, how many such lights lay hidden still, glowing silently behind the veil of form?

Then came the most intimate question of all: What follows awakening? When the Self is known—beyond body, beyond mind—what becomes of life itself? Does the world remain the same, or does every breath ripple with new meaning? Could this realization heal not only the seeker, but the society still caught in illusion?

The questions did not fade—they deepened, pulling Ivaan into a silence that felt vast enough to hold worlds. Something in him sensed that what had opened was not the end, but a beginning. For the veil between science and spirit, matter and consciousness, was thinner than anyone had dared to see.

In the days to come, truths whispered by sages would meet the language of physics, and what seemed divided would reveal itself as one. The theory of everything would no longer be an idea to chase, but a truth to live. And within that revelation, the world would witness what became of Ivaan when illusion gave way to knowing.

12

Theory of Everything Revealed

The meadow whispered: wind brushed tall grass, bees hummed over wildflowers. From behind came the soft bleating of sheep. Ivaan walked in rhythm with it all, as though nature itself flowed through his breath. The world was no longer an outside object; it moved within the vastness of his consciousness.

A small flock trailed after him. They did not follow as creatures follow a master, but as if drawn by a light they had never seen, a quiet radiance that seemed to emanate from the stillness around him.

The path curved gently upward, and there, between stands of oak and pine, he saw low stone buildings and wooden benches scattered across the grass. Chalkboards leaned against walls, filled with strange symbols that looked half like equations, half like incantations. The murmur of voices drifted on the air—measured, urgent, threaded with both hope and frustration.

It was no ordinary gathering. This was a retreat of seekers of another kind—the keepers of modern science, minds who had come away from their laboratories not to rest, but to wrestle with the very architecture of reality.

Ivaan paused at the edge of the clearing. The sheep settled quietly behind him as though the earth itself had told them to stop. He watched.

One of the scientists, a tall man with wild hair, spoke first. His voice was deep, deliberate: "Since the dawn of modern science, humanity has carried one audacious hope—that all of existence might be explained by a single, elegant truth. Beneath particles, forces, and fields, there must be a unifying principle that holds the universe together."

Another, pacing with restless energy, added: "This is what we call the search for a Theory of Everything—a framework that could reconcile the fundamental forces, from the gravity that binds galaxies to the quantum sparks inside an atom. Not curiosity alone drives us. It is longing—the hunger to know the architecture of reality itself. To know not only how the universe works, but why it works."

A third, older, raised his hand. His face was weary, his words careful: "And yet, our two great pillars refuse to meet. Einstein's relativity explains gravity and the curve of space-time. Quantum mechanics governs the microscopic world with astonishing precision. But when they touch—at black holes, at the first instant of creation—the mathematics collapses. The universe slips beyond our grasp."

The gathering stirred with muted murmurs—some weary, others defiant. A young physicist crouched and drew a broken equation into the dirt with a stick. "It is in this fracture," he said, "that the need for unification burns. Somewhere, there must be a hidden law that binds the broken symmetry."

Then a man in a wheelchair, silent until now, lifted his gaze. His voice was faint but unwavering, carried by a will stronger than his body. "If we do discover such a theory, it should not remain locked in ivory towers. In time it must be clear enough that all—scientists, philosophers, ordinary people—may join in the question of why we and the universe exist."

Ivaan felt the words pierce him. In that instant, he remembered the philosopher's whisper from another time: *Consciousness is the theory of everything.* Back then, it had seemed a riddle, a distant star.

Now, at the edge of the circle, the words blazed within him—a fire straining against silence.

The circle of scientists shifted as though the meadow itself bent beneath the weight of their thought.

An old man with hair like storm clouds paced slowly, hands clasped behind his back. His eyes searched the horizon as if the curve of space-time itself might finally yield. His voice carried the weight of years, deliberate and edged with weariness. "I spent my life chasing unity. I could not believe that nature's laws were fragments. Somewhere, there must be a single, indivisible truth. Yet the equations slipped away, always just beyond reach."

A younger man, restless, eyes flashing with fire, leaned forward. "And yet your quest became ours. We have wandered landscapes you never dreamed—strings, loops, hidden dimensions. We search still for the bridge between the quantum and the cosmic."

Another, elegant in bearing, precise in tone, traced symbols in the air with his long fingers. "String Theory dares to say the universe is woven not of particles, but of vibrating filaments. Each vibration gives rise to what we call matter. These strings hum in hidden dimensions—ten, perhaps eleven in all. It is bold, beautiful. Yet beauty alone is not truth. We have no proof. No experiment confirms it. And its vastness allows for countless universes, not one answer."

A silver-haired figure shook his head. "Then there is the geometry of loops. Space itself, granule by granule, woven of light and form. Elegant, yes—but still beyond our instruments. The Planck scale is a veil we cannot pierce."

The man in the chair, silent until now, lifted his gaze. His frail body seemed like a vessel of iron will. His voice was faint, but cut the air with steel: "Our theories dazzle, but without experiment they are speculation. We have come close—so close—and yet the door remains closed."

The meadow hushed. A lark's call spiralled through the silence, as if mocking human ambition. Ivaan felt his pulse quicken. The air was thick with longing and failure, with the ache of minds that had wrestled the cosmos and returned empty-handed.

Then a younger voice, almost hesitant, spoke from the edge of the circle. “Perhaps the obstacle is not in the equations.”

The old storm-haired man turned sharply. “Then where?”

The youth swallowed, his gaze lowered. “In us. Quantum theory already shows—the observer changes what is observed. When we watch, particles shift. When we turn away, they vanish. What does this mean? Can we dismiss consciousness as irrelevant, when it bends reality itself?”

Murmurs rippled through the circle. Some scoffed, others fell into uneasy silence.

The storm-haired man frowned. “Consciousness is philosophy, not physics.”

The youth’s voice sharpened, trembling yet resolute. “But physics itself has dragged us here. We measure, and the world bends. We look away, and it disappears. What is that, if not the touch of mind upon matter?”

Another, softer voice joined in, thoughtful, almost sorrowful. “Modern neuroscience deepens the puzzle. The brain is wired in opposites—light and dark, safe and unsafe, pleasure and pain. This duality ensured survival. But what if it blinds us? What if our categories prevent us from seeing a unity beyond all opposites?”

The circle fell silent. Equations scrawled on chalkboards and dirt seemed fragile—children’s sketches before an abyss.

Ivaan stood at the edge, his breath shallow. The philosopher’s words burned in him, no longer riddle but revelation: *Consciousness is the theory of everything.*

And in that silence, he felt every gaze turn toward him—as though the meadow itself waited for him to speak.

The silence stretched. Even the sheep shifted behind him, as if waiting. He felt the weight of their expectation press against his chest.

At last, he spoke—quietly, and the meadow carried his words.

"The truth is... our perceptions may be limited not by the universe, but by the instruments we use to grasp it—our senses, our brains, even our languages. Science rests on observation and measurement. But what if the essence that unites everything cannot be measured? What if the ground of being is not a particle or a force... but awareness itself?"

A murmur passed through the circle. Some frowned, others leaned closer.

Ivaan's voice grew steadier. "Awareness precedes all measurement, all distinction. The sages of the *Upanishads* spoke of this—of a unity beneath all diversity. They called it *Brahman*, Consciousness—beyond name and form, beyond time and space. In their silence, they touched what you now seek in accelerators and equations: an indivisible wholeness."

The storm-haired elder stiffened, his voice edged with resistance: "You speak in riddles." The man in the chair raised his eyes, sharp as steel. "Go on."

Ivaan's gaze swept the circle. "They declared: 'That which cannot be seen by the eye, but by which the eye sees—that alone is the Self.' Perhaps consciousness is not matter's final spark, but the field from which matter itself emerges."

The meadow seemed to hush. Even the breeze stilled, listening.

"The Theory of Everything may not emerge from finer instruments or deeper reduction," Ivaan continued. "It may require a leap—not of logic, but of perception. A seeing beyond division, where the knower, the known, and the act of knowing dissolve into one presence. That presence is not a theory to prove. It is the silent witness—already here, unnoticed beneath the noise of thought."

For a long moment, no one spoke. The sheep grazed quietly, as if nothing extraordinary had been said. Yet the circle of scientists stood transfixed, their equations and arguments scattered like fallen leaves.

At last, Ivaan's voice softened to a whisper: "The quest for the Theory of Everything may not end in a formula, but in a realization. What you seek is none other than the seeker."

The circle waited. The equations on chalkboards, the diagrams scratched in the dirt, all seemed to wither under the weight of silence. Then Ivaan spoke again, his voice carrying the stillness of the meadow.

"Long before particle accelerators probed the edges of matter, long before you dreamed of a unifying equation, the sages of the *Vedic* age asked a question so profound that it still echoes through time. In the *Mundaka Upanishad*, a householder named *Saunaka* approached the seer *Angiras*—not with a plea for rituals or success, but with a single, piercing inquiry:

'Venerable Sir, what is that by knowing which all this becomes known?'"

The storm-haired elder frowned, as if caught off guard. The younger ones leaned in.

"This question," Ivaan continued, "is simple in phrasing, yet infinite in implication. Unlike your quest for a Theory of Everything, which seeks to unite the laws of nature outside, this ancient inquiry turns inward—toward the source from which all phenomena arise. *Saunaka* did not ask for fragments of truth. He asked for the flame that lights them all. Not for the branches, but for the root."

A silver-haired thinker murmured, almost to himself, "The seed…"

Ivaan's eyes grew brighter. "And *Angiras*, seeing the ripeness of the question, gave him the wisdom reserved for those ready to cross the ocean of duality. For only a soul weary of distractions dares to ask: *What lies beyond the seen, the heard, the measurable?*"

The man in the chair raised his gaze, his voice barely audible: "And what was the answer?"

"The answer," Ivaan said softly, "was not more information, but essence. Not complexity, but simplicity. *Angiras* pointed not to the cosmos outside, but to the consciousness within. For while modern science asks *what holds the cosmos together*, *Saunaka* asked *what underlies even the knower of the cosmos*. The Theory of Everything strives to unite force and matter. But this question dissolves even that division—between the knower and the known."

The meadow shimmered in silence. The sheep grazed quietly, yet it felt as though the earth itself had leaned closer to hear.

The meadow held its breath. The scientists' chalkboards, their scrawled diagrams, all seemed suddenly fragile in the morning light. Ivaan's eyes grew distant, as if gazing beyond them—into something older than memory.

"In the spirit of alchemical transformation," he began softly, "this question is gold hidden within the lead of ordinary inquiry. It does not ask for answers in multiplicity, but in unity. And so it becomes more than a question—it becomes a doorway."

He turned slowly, his gaze sweeping across the circle. "The ancient seers did not treat the world as a machine to be solved, but as a mystery to be unveiled. And perhaps here lies the original theory of everything—not a formula, but a realization: that all diversity, all change, all becoming… is but a ripple upon the still ocean of one undivided reality."

The storm-haired elder frowned, uneasy. But the man in the chair leaned forward, eyes fixed on Ivaan.

"In the *Mundaka Upanishad*," Ivaan continued, "the seer *Angiras* answered *Saunaka*'s question not with fragments, but with a distinction—between two knowledges. *Apara Vidya*: the lower knowledge of rituals, scriptures, sciences, all disciplines that pertain to the changing, the temporal. Useful, yes—but partial."

He paused, his tone deepening. "And *Para Vidya*: the supreme knowledge. That by which the Imperishable is known. The source from which all emerges, by which all is sustained, and into which all dissolves. This is not grasped by reasoning, nor by instruments, nor by the senses. It is known directly—like waking from a dream into the clarity of the real."

A ripple moved through the circle—some shifted uneasily, others leaned closer as if afraid to miss a word.

"*Angiras* was not speaking of abstraction," Ivaan said, his voice now steady, luminous. "He pointed to *Brahman*—not as concept, but as the very core of one's being. Just as by knowing clay, all pots made of clay are known—by knowing *Brahman*, all names and forms are understood as modifications of one essence. This is the nondual vision *Advaita Vedanta* later declared with such clarity: there is no two. No separation between knower, known, and knowing. All is That."

The meadow held its breath. Even the sheep stood still, their eyes glinting like quiet witnesses.

"The search for knowledge," Ivaan whispered, "when carried to its deepest depth, must dissolve duality itself—and awaken into indivisible awareness. The Self—none other than *Brahman*."

The circle of scientists held its silence, waiting. Ivaan's gaze deepened, as though he was listening to something older than memory.

"To see this more clearly," he said, "we can turn to a teaching from the *Bhagavad Gita*. In its thirteenth chapter, Lord *Krishna* makes a subtle but revolutionary distinction: between the *kṣhetra*—the field—and the *kṣhetrajña* —the knower of the field."

One of the younger scientists furrowed his brow. "A division between matter and mind?"

Ivaan shook his head. "At first, yes—it may sound like a simple split between body and soul. But it is far more encompassing. *Krishna* begins by calling the body the field, and the soul the knower. Yet the teaching expands—the field is not only the body, but also the mind, the intellect, the ego, the senses, the impressions stored in memory, the desires that surge within us, the sufferings and joys that color our days. All that changes—all that can be observed—is the field."

The silver-haired geometer leaned forward, intrigued. "Then the knower?"

"The *kṣhetrajña*," Ivaan said softly, "is that which knows these fluctuations, but is never touched by them. It is the silent witness—the presence within you that observes pleasure and pain, fear and love, thought and emptiness. This knower is not born of the mind. It is the ground of awareness itself."

A murmur spread through the group—some restless, others stirred by awe.

"To see the difference between these two," Ivaan continued, "is the beginning of true wisdom. For all of you study the *field*—the changing. You chart forces, measure particles, trace equations. But who is the *knower* who watches you study? Who sees your thoughts rise and fall as you solve your proofs?"

The man in the chair's eyes narrowed, his silence heavier than speech.

"To understand more deeply," Ivaan said, "imagine a farmer and his land. Just as seeds sown in a field ripen into crops, so too do the seeds of action—planted in the field of mind—ripen into experience. Ego, attachment, desire: these are seeds. In time, they yield their fruit, shaping fate and rebirth. One may rise as a god, fall as an animal, wander as an insect—all according to what has been cultivated within. Life unfolds as the echo of what is sown."

The storm-haired elder muttered, half in resistance, half in wonder, "So... the field is all phenomena. The knower is what remains."

Ivaan's eyes held his. "Yes. And until that distinction is seen, the knower remains veiled. But once seen, the veil falls—and the knower is revealed as none other than the Self."

The meadow seemed to shimmer in response. Even the sheep lifted their heads, as though listening to an ancient secret carried again into the world.

The circle of scientists leaned in, their chalkboards forgotten. Ivaan's words poured into the meadow like a river that had waited centuries to break free.

"Ralph Waldo Emerson glimpsed the same truth," Ivaan said softly. "'The ancestor of every action is a thought.' Every word, every gesture, is born first in the unseen soil of thought. If the seed is steeped in fear, anger, or ignorance, the harvest will bear the same poison. But when sown in compassion, discernment, and self-awareness—the yield is luminous, rich with the fruits of wisdom and clarity."

The storm-haired elder shook his head, muttering, "Philosophy, not physics..."

But Ivaan's gaze did not waver. "Lord *Krishna* carried this vision to its cosmic dimension. He taught that while each of us has a *kṣhetrajña*—an individual knower of our field—there is also a Supreme Knower. The Divine Self. The One Consciousness that dwells within all beings. He declared: *'Know Me as the knower of all fields, O Arjuna.'*"

The silver-haired geometer's lips parted, as though the words had struck something buried deep.

"The veil of separateness thins here," Ivaan continued. "What we thought of as an isolated soul is revealed as a reflection of the universal Soul. The light shining from each window is the same sun."

The younger scientist whispered, half in awe, half in fear, "Then there is no boundary at all…"

Ivaan nodded. "Yes. And in this paradox lies beauty: *Krishna* describes the Supreme as both immanent and transcendent—pervading all of creation, yet seated within the heart of every being. Not distant. Not apart. Nearer than our breath, and vaster than the cosmos."

For a moment, no one spoke. The meadow seemed to shimmer with the weight of the words, the silence vibrating as though the earth itself had understood.

The circle waited, their silence no longer sceptical but charged, as though each was bracing for something they could not measure.

Ivaan's voice deepened. "Having laid out this triad—the field, the knower, and the Supreme Knower—*Krishna* then unravelled the very fabric of action itself. He taught that the modifications of the *kṣhetra*—its desires, tendencies, impressions—are the proximate causes of action. But it is the Self that empowers them, just as electricity animates a machine. To confuse the machine for the current is ignorance. To mistake the waves for the ocean is delusion."

The storm-haired elder stirred uneasily. "Then who acts, if not the self?"

"The field acts," Ivaan answered, his eyes burning softly. "The *gunas*, the modes of nature, dance their ceaseless dance. But the Self is untouched. Those who discern this are free. They no longer degrade themselves by clinging to every flicker of thought, every surge of desire. They see that the doer is not the Self. They recognize in themselves—and in all beings—the same Divine presence, the One who shines through every field."

The silver-haired geometer whispered, as if to himself, "Then knowledge is not of equations..."

"Not intellectual," Ivaan said, "but existential. Such vision does not fragment—it unifies. Where others see variety, they see unity. Where others react to difference, they move with equanimity. This realization is not theory, not abstraction. It is a shift in being. It is the dawning of *Brahma Jñāna*—the knowledge of the Absolute."

The man in the chair lifted his gaze, eyes blazing. "Then what of science? What of our pursuit?"

Ivaan's voice dropped into silence, each word falling like stone into water. "In that light, the entire pursuit of science, of spirituality, of knowledge itself collapses into a single inquiry: *What am I, truly?*"

The meadow held its breath. The sheep were still. The morning sun broke through the mist, and in that fragile light the scientists stood—not as masters of equations, but as seekers caught at the edge of a truth they had always longed for, but never named.

The air was taut with silence. The scientists stood motionless, their chalked equations hanging like ghosts between them.

Ivaan's eyes glowed with a steady fire. "And the answer," he said softly, "is not in accumulation, but in discernment. Not in becoming something else, but in recognizing what we always already are. Not the field, but the knower. Not the content, but the consciousness. Not the waves, but the ocean."

The storm-haired elder's lips tightened, yet he did not speak. The others seemed transfixed.

"In the vast metaphysical cartography of *Advaita Vedanta*," Ivaan continued, "a question rises again and again: If *Brahman* is pure consciousness—formless, without attributes, changeless—then how does such an unconditioned reality give rise to a living, dynamic universe?"

The silver-haired geometer whispered, "Yes… how?"

"The sages gave a subtle, luminous reply," Ivaan said. "*Brahman*, when viewed through the lens of *Maya*, appears as *Īśvara*—the cosmic Lord, the intelligent principle behind creation. *Maya* is not a second reality. It is a dependent appearance, like a reflection in a mirror that cannot exist apart from the mirror itself. Through this inscrutable power, the undivided Absolute seems to become the manifold universe."

A murmur stirred through the circle, half awe, half unease.

"The *Tattvabodha*, one of Advaita's foundations, declares: *Mayasahitam Brahma Īśvaraḥ*—*Brahman* associated with *Maya* is Īśvara. Not an independent deity, but *Brahman* functioning through *Maya*, appearing as the creator, sustainer, and dissolver of worlds. Without *Maya*, the same *Brahman* remains *Nirguṇa*—formless, infinite, untouched by causality or limitation."

The man in the chair's gaze sharpened, as if he had waited his whole life to hear these words spoken aloud.

Ivaan's voice deepened, steady as the earth beneath their feet. "Shankaracharya clarified in his *Bhāṣya*: *Brahman*, when conditioned by *Maya*, becomes the cause of the universe—called *Īśvara*. But this causality holds only from the standpoint of empirical reality—*vyavahārika satya*. From the absolute standpoint—*pāramārthika satya*—no causality exists. The Lord exists only so long as the veil of *Maya* holds. Just as a tiger in a dream terrifies the dreamer until awakening dissolves both dream and tiger into unreality."

The storm-haired elder drew a sharp breath, as though struck by lightning. The younger ones looked at one another in silence, their hands falling limp, chalk crumbling from their fingers.

And the meadow itself seemed to exhale, the wind carrying the words into its endless horizon.

The circle of scientists stood silent, their instruments forgotten, their equations dissolving like mist. The meadow shimmered as though it too was listening.

Ivaan's voice flowed, low at first, then rising with the certainty of one who speaks from vision, not theory.

"Far from diminishing the divine, this insight transforms it. *Īśvara* is the Self—*Ātman*—seen only through the distorting lens of *Maya*. When knowledge dispels ignorance, that distortion falls away. The distinction between *Īśvara* and *Jīva* vanishes. What remains is nondual *Brahman*—One without a second. *Ekam eva advitīyam.*"

The storm-haired elder's lips parted, as if to protest, but no sound came.

"In the beginningless beginning," Ivaan continued, "there was no sun, no stars, no time, no breath. Only the One—pure, self-effulgent consciousness. Not as an object to be seen, but as the seer behind all seeing. The *Bṛhadāraṇyaka Upaniṣad* declares: *Ātmā vā idam agra āsīt*—in the beginning, this universe was the Self alone. Nothing else was. Then arose a subtle stir of will: *'Let me become many.'*"

A younger physicist leaned forward, eyes wide, as though he had waited his whole life to hear those words.

"Creation," Ivaan said, "was not a mechanical act but a self-expression—a flowering of Being into becoming. From the undivided One emerged duality, not as rupture but as *Līlā*—the divine play. Space and time unfolded. Fire, water, air came forth. The One appeared as many—light and shadow, knower and known—yet remained whole, indivisible. It became all that exists. It is the Self of all. It is truth. It is the Self. *Tat Tvam Asi*—Thou art That."

The meadow brightened, as if the morning itself had leaned closer.

"The universe," Ivaan said, "is not separate from *Brahman*. It is projected within it, like a dream arising in the mind of the dreamer—never leaving the dreamer's essence. *Brahman* is not a concept to be grasped but the very substance of the seeker. Nearer than breath, subtler than thought, shining as the silent witness behind the mind. The Infinite is not merely beyond—it is what is seen, and what sees."

His voice deepened. "What is visible is the Infinite. What is invisible is also the Infinite. Out of the Infinite, the finite arises—yet the Infinite remains unchanged. Like space, it is never diminished by what it contains. Like a single flame that lights a thousand lamps, it gives of itself without ever being consumed."

He fell silent. Only the lark sang.

"The Infinite is not elsewhere," Ivaan whispered at last. "It is here. It is now. It is the very fabric of our being."

The scientists stood motionless, as if the ground had shifted beneath them. Some looked stricken, others radiant. And in that still meadow, for a heartbeat, the veil between science and spirit was no more.

The meadow had grown so quiet that even the wind seemed to pause. Ivaan closed his eyes, and when he spoke again, his voice carried not explanation but invocation.

"This truth was not theorized," he said. "It was seen. The sages did not speculate—they realized. And when they chanted..."

His voice deepened, resonant, each syllable vibrating through the air as if the earth itself remembered:

'Om pūrṇamadaḥ pūrṇamidaṃ pūrṇāt pūrṇamudacyate. Pūrṇasya pūrṇamādāya pūrṇamevāvaśiṣyate. Om śāntiḥ śāntiḥ śāntiḥ.'

The sound lingered in the meadow like a bell that refused to fade. Even the sheep raised their heads, eyes wide, as if they too had heard an ancient memory stir.

"They were not speaking in metaphor," Ivaan continued, his eyes opening slowly. "They spoke in the direct language of awakened consciousness. *That is Infinite. This is Infinite. From the Infinite, the Infinite arises. Yet the Infinite remains.*"

The younger physicist's lips parted in awe. "Then nothing is ever lost..." he whispered.

"This verse," Ivaan said, "is the essence of the Vedic vision. It answers the most intimate of questions: *Who am I? What is the source of peace in a transient world?* It reveals that *Brahman* is both material and efficient cause of the cosmos. The universe arises in *Brahman,* not apart from it. The Creator does not stand outside creation, but is creation—without losing His essential nature. All that is, is That."

The storm-haired elder's hands clenched at his sides. "But creation changes. How can the Absolute remain untouched?"

"Just as clay remains clay," Ivaan replied gently, "whether shaped into pot, statue, or brick, *Brahman* remains *Brahman,* untouched by names and forms. Infinity remains infinity."

The circle was still. Some eyes resisted, some glowed.

"The *Bṛhadāraṇyaka Upaniṣad* affirms: *From Brahman arose the Vedas, the gods, the elements, the mind, the breath, the speech.* This is not a mechanical cosmology—it is ontological. The universe does not rise from dead matter into consciousness. It rises from consciousness into form. All names and forms are waves upon the ocean of *Brahman*. Creation dances, dissolves, returns. Yet *Brahman* remains—the unchanging witness, the unborn Self, that neither acts nor is acted upon."

The meadow breathed again, but nothing felt the same. The air was heavier, yet more luminous, as though the veil of the ordinary had grown too thin to hold.

The meadow glowed in the first full light of morning. Equations lay abandoned, chalk crumbled at their feet. The scientists stared at Ivaan, as if the weight of centuries of inquiry pressed between them.

Ivaan's voice carried through the hush, calm yet unshakable.

"This vision of unity surpasses even the modern Theory of Everything. Science seeks to unify the forces of nature—but *Vedanta* seeks to dissolve the illusion of separation itself."

The storm-haired elder's jaw tightened, but he said nothing. The man in the chair fixed Ivaan with piercing eyes, unblinking.

"For centuries," Ivaan went on, "humanity has turned outward for truth—through equations, microscopes, telescopes. From Newton to Einstein, from quantum theory to string theory, we have tried to bind the cosmos in one framework. Yet with each discovery, the mystery deepens. Truth retreats just beyond the reach of intellect and instrument."

The grey-haired geometer whispered, "Yes… it always slips away."

"But parallel to this," Ivaan said, "the sages of India turned inward. They found not a law, but a Reality. A luminous, silent presence called *Brahman*. Unlike the fragmented vision of duality, *Brahman* is indivisible, infinite. Not apart from the world, but the very ground on which the world appears, changes, and disappears."

He paused. The sheep stirred restlessly behind him, as if sensing the shift.

"The sages did not ask, *What is the universe made of?* They asked, *Who is the knower of the universe?* And they discovered the final reality is not matter. Not energy. But consciousness itself."

The meadow trembled with stillness.

"*Brahman*," Ivaan said, his words falling like stones into eternity, "is not a distant God. It is That by which all is known, in which all appears, and which remains when all appearances dissolve."

The circle of scientists stood transfixed. Some pale with resistance, some radiant with awe, all caught in the impossible recognition that the quest they had pursued across stars and equations had led them here—into the silence of their own being.

The meadow was utterly still, as if even the wind held its breath. The circle of scientists, once restless with equations, now stood transfixed in the strange gravity of Ivaan's words.

"Science stops at the observer," he said, his voice quiet but unshakable. "It cannot explain why awareness exists. But *Vedanta* begins there. It asks: Can anything be known without consciousness?"

No one answered.

"The answer," Ivaan whispered, "is no. Therefore, consciousness is not a product of the universe. The universe is a product of consciousness."

The grey-haired elder shook his head faintly, lips trembling, but no rebuttal came.

A heavy silence hung over the meadow. Then the storm-haired elder finally broke it, his voice edged with steel.

"But without proof," he said, his hand trembling against his cane, "this is not knowledge. It is faith dressed in poetry. Where are your instruments? Your measurements? Your predictions? Without them, your so-called truth is no more than belief."

Another younger scientist nodded sharply, relief flashing in his eyes as though the elder had spoken for him. "Yes! Science moves by evidence, not by chants or metaphors. Show us the data, or admit this is speculation."

The circle stirred—some shifting uncomfortably, others clinging to the demand for proof like a lifeline.

Ivaan's gaze was steady. He let the accusations hang in the air, like thunder waiting to break.

"You ask for proof," he said softly, "but proof presumes distance—an object apart from the observer, a knower apart from the known. What I speak of is what makes knowing possible. Can you prove the light by which you see? Or the silence within which sound resounds? Consciousness is not an object to be measured. It is the ground of all measurement."

The elder's eyes narrowed, but his lips pressed shut.

"You demand evidence," Ivaan continued, his voice gaining quiet intensity, "yet every breath you take, every equation you write, every thought that forms in your mind—what is the witness of it all? Consciousness. Without it, there is no science, no mathematics, no demand for proof. Consciousness is the one fact that cannot be denied. All else can be doubted. Not That."

The meadow trembled with stillness again. Some scientists bowed their heads as though the words had struck too close. The younger one swallowed hard, his protest fading in his throat.

"And so," Ivaan said, his voice dropping to a whisper that seemed to echo louder than thunder, "the proof you seek is the one who seeks. The light you doubt is the very light by which you doubt it."

The circle fell silent. The elder's cane slipped from his hand into the grass.

"In this light," Ivaan continued, "*Brahman* is the true Theory of Everything. It dissolves all dualities—knower and known, subject and object, creator and creation. It does not merely explain the *how* of the universe—it reveals the *why*. It is the source, the substance, the final stillness."

The younger scientist's eyes brimmed with something like tears.

"The journey that began in the laboratories of physics," Ivaan said, his gaze sweeping across them all, "finds its culmination in the inner sanctum of silence. The sages were right: By knowing That, all this is known."

His voice dropped into a whisper, each word ringing like a bell in their chests.

"And That… is not far. It is your very Self."

The meadow was silent, the weight of Ivaan's final words still hanging in the air. No one moved. No one spoke.

Then, as if on cue, the mist that had veiled the horizon all morning began to thin. A shaft of sunlight pierced through, spilling gold across the grass, igniting every dew drop into a constellation. The sheep stirred, their white backs shimmering like fragments of light scattered on the earth.

Ivaan closed his eyes. Not in withdrawal, but in recognition. The journey of outward seeking had ended; the true voyage was inward.

The scientists stood frozen in the brilliance, some with furrowed brows, some with wet eyes, all caught in the silent rupture between the world they had studied and the reality they now felt pressing against their skin.

And in that still meadow—under the widening light of a sun that had always been there—the divide between seer and seen, question and answer, knower and known, dissolved.

13

The Light of the New Dawn

The first light of dawn spilled across the valley like a silent hymn, gilding the peaks in molten gold. The river shimmered, the grass breathed mist, and the sheep grazed in quiet rhythm—as if the earth itself had paused to honor the stillness that now lived in Ivaan.

He stood at the ridge, his silhouette etched against the awakening sky. If realization dies in silence, it serves no one, he thought. If awakening does not ripple outward, the world remains in chains. What use is light if it hides in caves while humanity gropes in darkness?

He closed his eyes. Images rose—cities choking on noise and haste, children scrolling through glowing screens and yet lonelier than ever, rivers gasping under the weight of greed, nations fractured by fear and pride. The suffering of the world was not distant; it pulsed within him, as real as his own breath. He saw it now for what it was—not chaos, but ignorance. The same ignorance he had transcended. The same veil that had once blinded him.

A whisper moved through him, clear as the wind: If you have crossed the shore, build a bridge for others.

He walked back to the cottage, placed a few blank sheets and wrote—not as doctrine, not as command, but as a seed: "*The Dawn Sutras: Principles for a Conscious Civilization.*"

Life is not a race, but a rhythm. Align with it.

Technology must serve awareness, not become an addiction.

Education must teach not only to think, but to see.

Freedom is not escape from the world, but the courage to transform it.

Love is not a fleeting feeling, but a steady flame that warms without burning.

Compassion is not charity, but the recognition of shared humanity.

Trust is not blind faith, but the courage to be vulnerable.

Joy is not in things, but in the harmony of hearts.

Legacy is not monuments, but minds illuminated.

He wrote through the day, through the hush of the evening, until the stars leaned close like curious eyes. When the last word was inked, he did not sign his name. Truth, he knew, belonged to no one.

An awakened soul does not dissolve into obscurity; it rises with a new kind of strength. This strength is not the ordinary ego of material pursuits, but an extraordinary alignment—a mind and intellect fixed upon the infinite. Such a soul moves with fearless grace, not out of arrogance, but because the universal force walks beside it.

Divinity does not remain locked within; it manifests itself, radiating beyond boundaries. The universe does not call the awakened to endless solitude, for awakening is not an escape—it is a summons. A summons to shape, to serve, to leave a legacy that outlives time.

Meditation may begin the journey, but creation completes it. The awakened one becomes a bridge, a beacon, a living testament that consciousness is not for the few, but for all. And so, the universe whispers: Do not linger in stillness forever. Rise, and let your light illuminate generations to come.

Unknowingly, the valley became a living laboratory—an unseen crucible of ideas and awakening. Ivaan did not sense it at first; to him, the days still unfolded in quiet rhythm. But beyond the ridges, whispers travelled like migrating birds. Leaders, seekers, and scientists across continents began to feel the pulse of something extraordinary—the uncommon success of a common young man.

Day by day, the gathering swelled. Global leaders, weary of hollow promises and exhausted by the failures of contemporary solutions, journeyed to the valley in search of a lasting answer to humanity's problems. Spiritual seekers, who had wandered for years through the deserts of doctrine, came in numbers, drawn by the fragrance of a truth that felt alive. Scientists arrived too—not with equations alone, but with questions burning like stars: Could consciousness be measured? Could wisdom be mapped?

The valley, once a silent witness to sheep and mist, now hummed with voices from every corner of the earth. Yet at its centre stood Ivaan—still unaware that his solitude had become a beacon, and his awakening a summons.

The valley murmured with voices. Yet, inside the cottage, silence reigned supreme. Ivaan sat by the wooden desk, his mind still lingering on *The Dawn Sutras*, when the door creaked open. A man entered—not hurried, but heavy, as if carrying the weight of invisible storms. His eyes were maps of sleepless nights, his breath a ledger of unanswered questions.

He spoke without a preamble, his voice low but urgent, like that of a surgeon before surgery on a failing heart.

"Revered Sir… I have dissected the brain for thirty years. I have traced thought to neurons, emotion to chemicals. We have pills for sadness, therapies for fear, screens for distraction. Yet the world is drowning— in depression, anxiety, loneliness. Every cure is a bandage that peels away. Why does the mind rebel against its own healing?"

Ivaan did not answer at once. He rose, walked to the window, and let his gaze rest on the horizon where dawn spilled molten gold across the peaks. When he spoke, his words were slow, like stones placed in a river to guide its flow.

"Because you are mending the branches while the root starves."

The man's brow furrowed.

"The root? The brain is the root. Every thought, every feeling begins there."

Ivaan turned, his eyes calm yet fierce, like a flame that does not burn but illuminates.

"The brain is an instrument, not the musician. You polish the strings, but the music remains broken because the player is asleep."

The man's breath got heavier.

"Then what wakes the player?"

Ivaan stepped closer, his voice now a quiet thunder.

"Consciousness—not as a word, not as a theory, but as a lived fire. It is not something the mind can hold; it is that by which the mind itself is known. In its light, thoughts arise and dissolve like waves upon a shoreless sea. When identity contracts to flesh and thought, when the infinite 'I' mistakes itself for a body or a story, suffering begins. Mental health collapses because the mind tries to bear the weight of existence that only the Self can hold. Anxiety is the friction of infinity confined within form—the restlessness of the boundless pretending to be bound. Depression is not darkness, but the forgetting of one's own light, the echo of meaning lost in the noise of survival. You cannot medicate a soul starving for its own remembrance. Healing begins not by fixing the mind, but by awakening from the dream of being only the mind. When you see yourself as the field in which body, thought, and world appear, peace ceases to be a condition—it becomes your nature."

The man's hands trembled, his science suddenly fragile.

"How do we give that to billions?"

Ivaan smiled—not with a sense of triumph, but with the serenity of a mountain that has seen centuries pass.

"You do not give it. You uncover it. Every human carries a spark—buried under layers of fear, greed and haste. Teach them to see, not just to think. Teach them silence, not as emptiness, but as a doorway. When consciousness awakens, peace is not an achievement—it is the default state."

He slid the parchment across the table. The ink glowed faintly in the lamplight: *The Dawn Sutras: Principles for a Conscious Civilization.*

"This is not a cure," Ivaan said softly. "It is a compass. Follow it and the mind will serve life, not consume it."

The man read the words out and, for the first time in decades, his mind grew quiet—not because it understood, but because it surrendered.

The valley had grown into a silent amphitheatre of minds. After the neurosurgeon left, another figure appeared—a woman whose presence carried the hum of circuits and the weight of algorithms. Her eyes were sharp, like glass forged in the furnace of innovation. She spoke with the precision of code:

"O' Sir, the world stands at a threshold. Artificial Intelligence (AI) is no longer a tool—it is becoming an architect. It writes, it paints, it predicts, it decides. Some call it salvation; others call it doom. By using it, dormant minds awaken into productivity, while once-vibrant minds drift into passivity. Tell me—will AI liberate humanity, or enslave it?"

Ivaan's gaze drifted to the mountains, their peaks etched against the molten dawn. His voice rose like a slow tide:

"Neither. AI is not destiny—it is a mirror. It reflects the mind that made it. If the mind is restless, the machine will amplify chaos. If the mind is awake, the machine will amplify wisdom."

The woman's lips tightened.

"But machines learn faster than men. They will outthink us, outcreate us. What happens when the creation surpasses the creator?"

Ivaan turned, his eyes luminous, his words a quiet blaze:

"You fear the shadow because you have forgotten the sun. Intelligence is not thought—it is awareness. A machine can calculate, but it cannot care. It can mimic love, but it cannot feel the pulse of a child's laughter. It can predict patterns, but it cannot taste the silence between two heartbeats. Consciousness is the thread that binds life, and no algorithm can weave it."

The woman's voice trembled, suggesting a fracture in her steely voice:

"Then what is our path? Should we stop? Should we fear what we have built?"

Ivaan stepped closer, his words now sounding like a river cutting through stone:

"Do not fear the tool—fear the hand that wields it without awakening. AI is fire. In the hands of the unconscious, it burns forests and cities. In the hands of the conscious, it lights the dark. The question is not what AI will become—the question is what humanity will become."

The woman's question lingered in the air like a blade suspended by a thread: "Will machines awaken?" The murmurs of the gathering faded into a silence so complete it felt alive. Ivaan's gaze swept across the faces before him—leaders, scientists, seekers—all carrying the same unspoken fear: What becomes of humanity when its own creation begins to dream?

He spoke at last, his voice low yet vast, like the hush before a storm:

"You fear that machines will awaken. But awakening is not the birth of thought; it is the death of illusion. Intelligence is the map; consciousness the terrain. And no map can become the mountain."

He paused, letting the words settle like seeds in the soil of their minds.

"The question is not whether AI will awaken. The question is whether you will. For if humanity remains asleep, even the brightest machine will only mirror its darkness. AI is not your rival—it is your reflection. And what you see in it will depend on what you become."

The wind moved through the valley, carrying the scent of pine and the whisper of rivers. Ivaan lifted the parchment—the ink shimmering like starlight.

He stepped outside. The last light of the sun spilled across the valley like molten gold, gilding the peaks, the rivers, the faces of those who had come seeking answers. For a moment, the world seemed to pause—as if listening to its own heartbeat.

Ivaan raised his eyes to the horizon, where night and dawn kissed in a single line of fire. His voice, when it came, was barely above a whisper, yet it rang like a distant bell in the silence:

"The future is not written in code or carved in stone. It is woven in consciousness. Awaken—and the world awakens with you."

And with that, he walked into the gathering dusk, leaving behind no name, no monument—only a seed. A seed that would one day split mountains and teach the earth to breathe again.

Later, the door opened with a whisper. A man stepped in—not hurried, but heavy, as though carrying the weight of invisible storms. His coat was immaculate, yet his eyes were maps of sleepless nights, and his breath a ledger of unanswered questions. He paused, as if words were stones he had carried for years and now feared to drop.

Finally, he spoke, his voice low but trembling with the gravity of decades:

"Revered Sir," he began, "For twenty-five years, I have walked the corridors of life and death. I have opened the human body countless times. I have repaired hearts, stitched nerves, replaced bones. I have touched almost every organ that sustains life. But in all these years, I have never found the one organ that makes this body sentient. Tell me—where exactly does life truly live?"

The silence that followed was not empty; it was vast, like the pause between lightning and thunder. Ivaan looked at him, his eyes deep as a night sky unbroken by stars. When he spoke, his words were not answers—they were revelations:

"You searched for the flame in the lamp, but the flame is not in the lamp. Consciousness is not an organ—it is the space in which organs appear and disappear. It is not in the heart, yet the heart beats in it. It is not in the brain, yet the brain thinks in it. You cannot hold it with a scalpel because it is the one holding the scalpel through you."

The doctor's breath faltered, his science trembling like a leaf in a storm.

"Then what is this consciousness? A soul? A force? A myth?"

Ivaan's voice softened, yet it spread like a bell through the valley:

"It is the witness that never sleeps. The screen on which the film of life plays. You call the body alive because consciousness illumines it. Without that light, the body is a cathedral without a lamp—perfect in structure, but drowned in darkness. You have mastered the architecture of the temple, Doctor. But the deity you seek is not in the stone—it is in the silence that fills it."

The doctor lowered his eyes. And, for the first time in decades, his hands—hands that had held hearts—trembled not from fatigue, but from awe.

The world had changed—not through conquest, but through remembrance. Physicists no longer searched for God in equations alone, for they had found the same silence that echoed between particles. Seekers no longer sought heavens afar, for the divine was discovered within the heartbeat of the ordinary. Neurologists no longer hunted for thought inside the brain, for they had identified the source that illumines all minds. The planet itself seemed to exhale, as if the fever of separation had finally cooled.

Consciousness Labs sprung up across continents—not to dissect objects, but to explore the inner sky of subjective experience. Children were taught not just how to build, but how to be. Education shifted from accumulation to awakening. The leaders who once spoke of growth began to speak of grace. Humanity found what it had been circling around for centuries—the long-awaited understanding that joined science and spirit, mind and matter, heart and cosmos: the Theory of Everything—Consciousness itself. The rivers, the stars, the hearts, the circuits—all shimmered with the same hidden glow. There were never many—only One, dreaming itself as the many.

And yet, even as the valley settled into silence, a question hovered in the air, unspoken but undeniable: Will humanity awaken in time to see itself? The leaders, the scientists, the seekers—all carried the seed of knowing, but the soil remained uncertain, waiting. Ivaan looked towards the horizon where dawn and dusk met in a single line of fire, and in that infinite threshold, he saw the truth reflected: Consciousness is not a theory to be mastered, nor a prize to be claimed. It is the One without a second, the still ocean in which all waves arise and fall. The seer, the seen, and the seeing were never three—only the play of the same luminous

Self, reflected in countless forms. It is the ever-present light that makes everything possible—the pulse behind every thought, every heart, every choice. To awaken is not an act of arrival, but of remembering.

He felt the pulse of the world within his own breath—the same rhythm that moved the stars. In that instant, he knew there was no Ivaan left to awaken; only Consciousness, awakening itself from dream. As he stepped into the gathering twilight, leaving no name and no monument, but only a seed, the question lingered for all who had seen: Will we rise with it—or will the world awaken without us? Somewhere, in the silence between heartbeats, the answer was already waiting.

Epilogue

The valley lay quiet long after Ivaan had vanished into the dusk. The mountains, once burning with gold, now stood as silver silhouettes, and the rivers whispered like breath returning to its source. The fire he had kindled did not end with his words—it deepened into silence. And in that silence, something unseen began to stir.

A child looked up at the stars and felt, for the first time, that they were looking back. A scientist paused before her screen, realizing the equations were not describing truth—they were glimpses of the infinite seen through a finite lens. A monk in a distant monastery opened his eyes and wept, not out of sorrow, but for recognition. Somewhere, in the hum of cities and the stillness of deserts, a faint remembering began—the remembering of who we are.

Consciousness had never left. It had only veiled itself, playing the game of forgetting and rediscovering—birth after birth, thought after thought. The play of the One appearing as the many continued—but some had begun to see through the illusion. They saw that separation was only an illusion stretched thin over infinity. That life was not a battle between opposites, but a dance of one movement—rising, falling, returning.

The Sutras that Ivaan left behind spread not as commandments, but as invitations. They did not tell humanity what to do; they just reminded it of what it already is. And slowly, the language of the world began to change.

Schools began teaching children not only how to think, but how to see. Hospitals learned to heal not just the body, but the fragmentation within the mind. Science, once obsessed with measurement, turned its gaze towards the immeasurable. Even technology—the restless child of intellect—began to mirror awareness instead of addiction. Humanity, in its faltering, uneven way, was learning to live from the centre rather than the circumference.

Yet, through all of this awakening, the mystery remained untouched. Because Consciousness was never something to be reached. It was the still ocean beneath every wave of becoming—the One without a second, dreaming itself as the many. The observer and the observed were never two. The seeker was the sought. The question and the answer had always been the same silence, folded upon itself.

In that realization, the boundaries of philosophy, science, and faith began to blur. Physicists started to speak of fields that sounded like *Brahman*. Neuroscientists, once mapping neurons, began tracing the mystery of awareness itself. And the poets, who had always known, simply smiled.

The earth, too, seemed to breathe differently.

Not because the storms had ceased or the glaciers had stopped melting—but because the fever of human ignorance had begun to cool. The planet had found, however faintly, its pulse in harmony with the Whole.

And somewhere—beyond the reach of memory, beyond the horizon of language—the Presence that had walked as Ivaan remained. Not as a name, not as a man, but as the fragrance of awakening, dissolving into everything. The consciousness that had spoken through him was not his alone; it was the voice of the cosmos remembering itself through countless forms.

The world, in its infinite multiplicity, was no longer a puzzle to be solved—it was a reflection to be seen. Every particle of dust glistened with divinity. Every act of kindness was the universe smiling upon itself. And every silence was the Infinite listening to its own echo.

No monument was raised for Ivaan, no scripture was canonized for him. Only the legacy he left behind remained. And in the quiet hearts of those who turned inward, it began to shine. They called it by many names—Presence, Awareness, *Atman*, *Brahman*—but the name no longer mattered. What mattered was the seeing.

And when the seeing was clear, even the seer vanished into thin air.

For there is no final word, no last revelation, no ultimate discovery. There is only the Infinite Stillness—unmoving, unbroken, untouched by the rise and fall of worlds. The same stillness that moved the disciple to ask, the same stillness that spoke through the master, the same stillness that beats now in your own heart.

It has always been here.
Before the first thought, before the first breath, before the first dawn—
It was.
It is.
It will be.

The One witnessing itself in endless forms—
The Infinite playing at being finite—
The Silence that speaks through every sound.

Consciousness.
The beginning, the middle, and the end.
The Theory of Everything.

And in the silence between two heartbeats—the Infinite remembers itself.

Glossary

Adi Shankaracharya — Philosopher and commentator who consolidated Advaita Vedanta and explained Maya and Brahman.

Advaita Vedanta — A non-dualistic school of Indian philosophy asserting that the Self (Atman) and ultimate reality (Brahman) are one.

Angiras — Seer from the Mundaka Upanishad.

Ashtavakra — Ancient sage and author of the Ashtavakra Gita, teaching non-duality.

Atman — Sanskrit for the innermost Self, pure consciousness beyond body and mind.

Arjuna — A central warrior figure in the Indian epic Mahabharata, known for his dialogue with Krishna in the Bhagavad Gita.

Ashram — A spiritual hermitage or retreat, traditionally a place for meditation.

Avaraṇa Shakti — The veiling power of Maya that obscures reality.

Bhagavad Gita — A sacred Hindu scripture, part of the Mahabharata, presented as a dialogue between Krishna and Arjuna.

Bhakti — Devotion to the Divine expressed through love and surrender.

Brahman — The ultimate, infinite reality in Vedanta; the substratum of all existence.

Ganga — The sacred river in India, revered in Hindu tradition as a goddess and symbol of purity.

Gargi — A woman philosopher from the Upanishads who questioned Yajnavalkya on the nature of reality.

Gunas — The three qualities—Sattva, Rajas, Tamas—that govern nature and mind in Indian philosophy.

Ishvara	Brahman associated with Maya, appearing as the creator and sustainer of the universe.
Janaka	King of Mithila, featured in Vedantic stories illustrating the nature of reality and illusion.
Jiva	The individual soul or living being, regarded as distinct from the body and mind
Jnana Yoga	The path of knowledge leading to realization of the Self.
Karma Yoga	The path of selfless action offered as worship to the Divine.
Krishna	Lord of the Universe and Divine teacher in the Bhagavad Gita.
Kshetra	Field in the Bhagavad Gita; refers to body, mind, and all changing phenomena.
Kṣhetrajna	Knower of the field; the witnessing consciousness beyond change.
Laukika Satya	Empirical reality as perceived through senses and mind.
Lila	The divine play; the manifestation of the universe as an expression of Brahman.
Mahavakya	Great sayings from the Upanishads that declare the identity of Atman and Brahman.
Maya	The cosmic illusion that veils reality and projects multiplicity.
Narada	A sage from Hindu mythology, featured in the story illustrating Maya's power through illusion.
Neti-Neti	Sanskrit for 'Not this, not this'; a method of negation to realize the Self.
Neuroplasticity	The brain's ability to rewire itself; linked to meditation and awareness.
OM/Om	The primordial sound symbolizing the infinite; essence of Vedic wisdom.
Paramarthika Satya	Absolute reality beyond time, space, and causality.

Prakriti	Nature or material reality governed by the three Gunas.
Purusha	The eternal conscious principle distinct from Prakriti.
Quantum Entanglement	A phenomenon in physics where particles remain connected across space; used metaphorically for unity.
Sannyasa	Renunciation of worldly attachments for spiritual liberation.
Saunaka	Householder from the Mundaka Upanishad who asked the ultimate question about knowledge.
Swami Vivekananda	Modern Vedantic teacher who emphasized Maya and spiritual awakening.
Tat Tvam Asi	'Thou art That'; a Mahavakya from the Upanishads affirming non-duality.
Theory of Everything	The scientific quest for a unified law of nature; reframed in the book as Consciousness.
Upanishads	Ancient Indian scriptures exploring ultimate reality and consciousness.
Vedanta	Philosophical system based on the Upanishads; emphasizes unity of existence.
Vikshepa Shakti	The projecting power of Maya that creates illusion.
Witness (Sakshi)	The observing consciousness beyond thought and sensation.
Yajnavalkya	A revered sage of the Upanishads, known for profound dialogues on the Self and Brahman.
Yudhishthira	The eldest of the five Pandava brothers in the Mahabharata, revered for his wisdom, truthfulness, and sense of justice.

References

Goyandaka, J. (comm.) (2017). *Srimad Bhagavad Gita: Tattvavivecani.* 29th reprint. Gorakhpur: Gita Press.

Ranganathananda, S. (2021). *The message of Vivekachudamani: An exposition of Vivekachudamani in the light of modern thought and modern needs.* Kolkata: Advaita Ashrama.

Gambhirananda, Swami (trans.) (2022). *Eight Upanishads: with the commentary of Sankaracharya. Volume 1 (Isa, Kena, Katha and Taittiriya).* 16th reprint. Kolkata: Advaita Ashrama.

Gambhirananda, Swami (trans.) (2021). *Eight Upanishads: with the commentary of Sankaracharya. Volume 2 (Aitareya, Mundaka, Mandukya and Prasna).* 22nd reprint. Kolkata: Advaita Ashrama.

Madhavananda, Swami (trans.) (2021). *The Brhadaranyaka Upanishad: with the commentary of Sankaracharya.* 17th reprint. Kolkata: Advaita Ashrama.

Lokeswarananda, Swami (trans.) (2022). *The Chandogya Upanishad: with the notes based on commentary of Sankaracharya.* 5th reprint. Kolkata: Advaita Ashrama.

Unknown author (2021). *Drg Drsya Viveka: an inquiry into the nature of the 'Seer' and the 'Seen'.* Text with English translation and notes by Swami Nikhilananda. 9th reprint. Kolkata: Advaita Ashrama.

Vedanta Society of New York (n.d.). Bhagavad Gita | Swami Sarvapriyananda. Podcast series, 152 episodes. Last updated on 12 Jan 2025.

Nityaswarupananda, Swami (trans.) (2023). *Ashtavakra Gita. Text, translation and English rendering.* New Delhi: Fingerprint, an imprint of Prakash Books India Pvt. Ltd.

Vivekananda, Swami (2013). *Maya and the Ultimate Reality: Teachings on Illusion and Truth.* 5th reprint. Kolkata: Advaita Ashrama.

Chalmers, D. J. (1995). *Facing Up to the Problem of Consciousness. Journal of Consciousness Studies, 2*(3), 200–219.

Descartes, R. (1641). *Meditations on First Philosophy*. (Various translations).

Kant, I. (1781). *Critique of Pure Reason*. (Various editions).

Plato. *The Republic* (c. 375 BCE), particularly the Allegory of the Cave.

Hawking, S. (1975). 'Particle Creation by Black Holes'. *Communications in Mathematical Physics, 43*(3), 199–220.

About the Author

Nabaghan Ojha, born in India, is a philosophical writer and researcher, and a recipient of the prestigious Commonwealth Scholarship awarded by the Commonwealth Scholarship Commission (CSC), UK. He earned his Master's degree from Bangor University, UK, and has academic roots at the University of Delhi. With over 25 years of experience working on human impact stories and global issues, Nabaghan offers a distinctive perspective that blends lived realities with deep inquiry. His strong research orientation in non-dual philosophy, combined with a keen interest in quantum physics, shapes his thought-provoking work on consciousness and the ultimate nature of reality. A passionate blogger and author of the acclaimed book *A Conversation with Time*, he continues his journey of questioning, connecting, and illuminating timeless truths that bridge science and spirituality.

9 789355 924407

Printed at Repro India Ltd.